COLLEGE
SUCCESS

FOR Students
With Learning
Disabilities

Second Edition

COLLEGE SUCCESS

FOR Students With Learning Disabilities

A Planning and Advocacy Guide for Teens With LD, ADHD, ASD, and More

Cynthia G. Simpson, Ph.D., and Vicky G. Spencer, Ph.D.

Routledge
Taylor & Francis Group

NEW YORK AND LONDON

First published in 2020 by Prufrock Press Inc.

Published 2021 by Routledge
605 Third Avenue, New York, NY 10017
2 Park Square, Milton Park, Abingdon, Oxon OX14 4RN

Routledge is an imprint of the Taylor & Francis Group, an informa business

Library of Congress Cataloging-in-Publication Data

Names: Simpson, Cynthia G., author. | Spencer, Vicky G., author.
Title: College success for students with learning disabilities : a planning
    and advocacy guide for teens with LD, ADHD, ASD, and more / Cynthia G.
    Simpson, Ph.D., and Vicky G. Spencer, Ph.D.
Description: Second edition. | New York, NY: Taylor & Francis, [2020] |
    Includes bibliographical references. | Summary: ""College Success for
    Students With Learning Disabilities" (2nd ed.) offers students the
    knowledge, guidance, and strategies they need to effectively choose a
    college, prepare for university life, and make the most of their
    collegiate experience"-- Provided by publisher.
Identifiers: LCCN 2020027488 (print) | LCCN 2020027489 (ebook) | ISBN
    9781646320455 (paperback) | ISBN 9781646320462 (ebook) | ISBN
    9781646320479 (epub)
Subjects: LCSH: Learning disabled--Education (Higher)--United
    States--Handbooks, manuals, etc. | College student orientation--United
    States--Handbooks, manuals, etc.
Classification: LCC LC4818.38 .S56 2020 (print) | LCC LC4818.38 (ebook) |
    DDC 371.91--dc23
LC record available at https://lccn.loc.gov/2020027488
LC ebook record available at https://lccn.loc.gov/2020027489

ISBN 13: 978-1-6463-2045-5 (pbk)

DOI: 10.4324/9781003233749

Dedication

We would like to dedicate this book to those individuals with disabilities who have chosen to follow the college dream and to those individuals who may not have realized that college was a possibility. May you find yourselves examining this opportunity and reaching your full academic potential.

We also would like to dedicate this book to our families. Our husbands and children have provided us with love, support, and continued words of encouragement. We could not have done it without you. Thank you!

Table of Contents

Acknowledgments

There are many people who have contributed to the process of writing this book. First and foremost, we would like to thank James Williams, Jared Romeo, Ricky Adams, and Angela Corbin for allowing us to share their stories about attending college as students with disabilities. Their words will allow others to realize their own potential and seek the services they need to be successful college students. We also would like to thank Ricky's parents, as well as Mark and his parents (whose names have been changed for privacy reasons), for sharing their experiences that show the differing perspectives that family members have in regard to the college success of students with disabilities. In addition, we would like to thank our colleagues, who have supported us through the writing process and encouraged us to move forward with our own dreams, including Nancy Taylor, M.S., a transition job coach, who verified the accuracy of the federal transition guidelines presented throughout the book. Special thanks to the student chapters of Council for Exceptional Children and Best Buddies International for their work with students with disabilities and their efforts in facilitating peer friendships during the high school years and welcoming college students with disabilities into their organizations and onto the college campus.

Introduction

College Planning for Students With Learning Disabilities and Other Special Needs

The high school years are an exciting time for you and your family as you begin to make plans for the future: *Will I get a job? Will I go to college? Where will I live? Will I have friends?* These are just a few of the questions that you must face, but the answers may not always be easily accessible if you have been identified as a student with special needs. Most high schools have career centers that provide students with a wealth of information on topics such as college information sessions, financial aid, scholarships, and required testing. In addition, an overwhelming amount of college-related mail is distributed to students throughout their high school years. Unfortunately, the information received does not specifically address students with disabilities or even what services are offered to help mediate the college planning process.

DOI: 10.4324/9781003233749-1

Background and Terminology

This book serves as a resource for you, your parents, teachers, and other professionals who will assist in the development of a strategic process that can be individualized for students with learning disabilities (LD), along with other disabilities, such as Attention Deficit/Hyperactivity Disorder (ADHD) and autism spectrum disorders (ASD), who are transitioning from high school to college (also referred to as postsecondary education). When we refer to *college* or *university*, these terms also include trade schools, technical schools, community colleges, and junior colleges.

In the previous edition of this book, Asperger's syndrome was specifically referred to as a standalone disability. In the fifth edition of the *Diagnostic and Statistical Manual of Mental Disorders* (*DSM-5*), Asperger's syndrome was no longer included (American Psychiatric Association, 2013). The definition of ASD now encompasses a continuum of mild to severe. In addition, Social Communication Disorder has been recognized in the *DSM-5*.

Throughout this book, we often use the word *disabilities* or *disability* in lieu of identifying a specific disability. Although the content of the book is geared toward students identified with disabilities, including students with anxiety disorders, current practices within the public school system and within the field of special education have led educators to identify students in two groups: those accessing the general education curriculum and those accessing an adapted curriculum. Keeping this in mind, note that the suggestions offered throughout this book relating to college success could apply not only to those students currently served under the Individuals With Disabilities Education Act (IDEA), but also those who receive adaptations to the general curriculum under a civil rights law. Section 504 of the Rehabilitation Act of 1973 is a civil rights law that prohibits discrimination based on disability. This law applies to public elementary and secondary schools, and institutions of higher education, although the law is not limited to just educational institutions. Section 504 is not part of special education. However, it is a formal plan developed to ensure that a student who has a disability identified under the law and is attending an elementary or secondary educational institution receives supports and accommodations that will increase their academic success and access to the learning environment.

Any testing data that were used as part of the student's Individualized Education Program (IEP) or Section 504 during the K–12 years may be used by the postsecondary institution to determine needed accommodations for the student's program of study. Some universities require more recent documentation, meaning the student must obtain an evaluation from qualified assessment personnel to get the necessary documentation for their disability.

Therefore, to limit this book to only those identified as having specific learning disabilities might leave the impression that students with other disabilities or students served under Section 504 would not benefit from the information presented throughout the book. Any students served under Section 504 or receiving special education services, regardless of the identified disability, will find helpful information for the transition process from high school to postsecondary education. This process has to begin at the secondary level or earlier so that the student is prepared to move into the college setting. Needless to say, the entire process can become quite daunting, so planning is essential.

Organization of the Book

This book provides a step-by-step guide that can be used to help you chart the path toward planning for a postsecondary education. Each chapter ends with resources, including helpful checklists. You may use these checklists to keep detailed records of your own planning process. The Resources chapter at the end of the book provides information on financial aid and additional college planning resources.

Finally, each chapter of this book includes an interview with four students who share their experiences as college students with disabilities. Each of the students attends or attended a 4-year university.

> During the development of the first edition of this book, James Williams was a 21-year-old senior pursuing a degree in special education. He was identified with Asperger's syndrome (now referred to as ASD) at the age of 12. James shares his experiences related to the content of each chapter and provides practical tips that guided him through the college process. Many changes have occurred in the last several years, with James completing his Ph.D., getting married, and entering a profession in which he is serving individuals with disabilities.

> Angela Corbin majored in early childhood education. She was diagnosed with a learning disability (specifically, a math disorder and a processing disorder) when she was 9 years old. Angela received services as a student with LD during her college years.

> Jared Romeo, a first-year college student majoring in cyber engineering, was identified as a student with ADHD when he was 5 years old and received support in school under 504.

> Ricky Adams was diagnosed with a learning disability when he was 10 years old. Ricky chose to begin his college career at a community college but transferred to a 4-year college after one year, where he received academic support to address his learning difficulties. He is now the head wrestling coach at a high school.

Each student's experiences while attending college offer insights as to the obstacles they faced, or continue to face, while attending college and how they worked to overcome the challenges presented to them. Readers, regardless of their role in the college planning process, will be able to use this book as a roadmap toward a successful college career.

Our Goals

The interest in writing this book began on a personal level. While teaching in the public school setting and at the college level, we met many students with disabilities who said they never pursued a college education because they did not realize that was an option for them. Some students stated that their teachers, school counselor, and parents never discussed the possibility of postsecondary education as a viable option. Other students said that they had begun a college education, but they were unaware of or unable to access the services they needed in order to be successful academically. Still other students were tired of being labeled with a disability in high school, so they chose not to self-identify once they were in college. Unfortunately, many of these students were unable to succeed without any supports in place. As parents, we knew this was a possibility that our own children could face.

It is our intent that this book be used as a resource that can inform you, as a student with a disability or a student needing modifications to the general curriculum, firstly, that you can pursue a college education; secondly, how to move forward with your goal of transitioning to college; and finally, that you are your own biggest advocate. Information is power, and we hope that we have provided the necessary information that you will need in order to advocate for yourself and have a successful college experience.

1

Making the Change

Transition Planning

Stephen Covey said, "to begin with the end in mind" (1989, p. 9). Although Covey wrote these words more than 30 years ago, this idea still holds true today in the world of transition planning. Beginning with the end in mind sets the educational course for students like you to move successfully from school to postsecondary education, vocational training, integrated employment, independent living, and community participation based on your preferences, interests, and abilities. Most students who are planning a college education begin the process during the high school years. However, for students with disabilities, that process will need to begin much earlier.

As a student with disabilities in the public school system, you are protected under certain laws that provide specific rights and responsibilities. However, once you have graduated from high school and move into a postsecondary institution, there are changes in the laws that will affect your rights and responsibilities, as well as the services that can be provided. It is important to know what these changes

DOI: 10.4324/9781003233749-2

are and to begin addressing them long before graduation from high school.

Ensuring that students with disabilities have access to and full participation in postsecondary education has become a major focus in secondary education and transition planning for students with disabilities. Postsecondary education is targeted as an important transition outcome for students with disabilities because of the impact of a college degree on future adult outcomes (Joshi & Bouck, 2017). The same holds true for a postsecondary certification program that may not be a degree pathway. Students with disabilities who graduate from college have employment rates and salaries comparable to their peers without disabilities (Kauffman et al., 2017). Thus, it seems imperative that students with disabilities, as well as their parents, teachers, and counselors, be well-informed on how to best prepare to pursue a postsecondary education, as well as learn the skills needed to be successful in that setting.

Over the past 2 decades, an increasing number of students with disabilities have chosen to pursue a postsecondary education. As of 2016, students with disabilities made up 11% of students pursuing a postsecondary education (Snyder et al., 2016). Unfortunately, when compared with their peers without disabilities, they are at a higher risk for experiencing academic, behavioral, and emotional demands that may have a negative impact on their college success (Henrickson et al., 2017). However, effective transition planning as young adults to address these possible barriers can improve postschool outcomes (Cimera et al., 2014). Being proactive and staying informed can also help students to avoid common mistakes that can be made during the postsecondary transition planning/evaluation process. Figure 1 outlines 10 common mistakes to avoid during postsecondary planning.

The impact of federal policy calling for transition planning in the 1997 and 2004 amendments to the Individuals With Disabilities Education Act (IDEA, 2004) has resulted in improved transition services and has had a positive effect on better preparing students with disabilities for life after high school (Newman, 2005). These changes have encouraged students with disabilities to consider all of their

Figure 1
Top 10 Mistakes to Avoid During Postsecondary Planning

Mistake #1: Goals Are Too Broad Goals are too broad and don't include the specific steps a student will need to take to reach the goal. **Example:** *Bob will go to college when he graduates.*
Mistake #2: Goals Are Too Specific Goals are too specific and focus on a minute detail that may not actually impact a student's functioning. **Example:** *Bob will not wear blue clothing more than three times a week.*
Mistake #3: Goals Disregard Student's Actual Functioning Goals are based solely on the student's or family's hopes, dreams, and/or interests without considering the student's current academic, physical, mental, or intellectual functioning. **Example:** *Bob wants to be a heart surgeon but has a third-grade reading level and would most likely not pass the MCAT to get admitted.*
Mistake #4: Goals Focus Solely on Academics Goals focus only on academics and do not include the other two domains mentioned in IDEA: postsecondary employment and independent living. IQ is not always a predictor of success. **Example:** *Bob is 17 years old and has a goal of successfully answering seven out of 10 algebra problems correctly, but his mother dresses and bathes him every day.*
Mistake #5: Goals Disregard Student's Local Job Market Goals do not consider the actual job market where the student lives or is willing to move and whether it's feasible that they can obtain a position with their training or degree. **Example:** *Bob has a BA in history because it's his hobby, but he doesn't want to teach. Teaching jobs are the most likely positions he can secure in his area.*

Figure 1, continued

Mistake #6: Goals Are Not Student-Centered Goals are based upon suggestion and influence from others and not necessarily the student's informed choice.
Example: *Bob's parents want him to be an accountant because it pays well and his dad is an accountant, so they send him to college for that, but he skips class due to lack of interest and doesn't pass anyway.*
Mistake #7: Goals Are Not Based Upon Vocational Evaluation Evidenced-based, functional vocational evaluation was either not conducted or was conducted by staff who lack the appropriate certification, licensure, or training.
Example: *Special education teacher training programs generally provide no training/coursework on teaching or evaluating transition or vocational skills; however, many schools unfairly ask teachers to conduct vocational assessments without providing any training or guidance on how to administer the testing or interpret the findings.*
Mistake #8: Insufficient Connection to Adult Services Connection to adult services providers/agencies was either not provided, or, if it was, the parent was not educated as to what the agencies provide, what their limitations are, and when parents should contact them.
Example: *Bob didn't get on the Medicaid Waiver waitlist until he was 18; once on the list, it takes 10 years to receive funding, so he won't have the services when he needs them most.*
Mistake #9: Lack of Parent Training Parents usually receive little, if any, training focused on preparing them for their child's graduation and the many changes that will occur regarding their legal, financial, and educational status.
Example: *Parents did not know their financial holdings and income will impact their child's ability to receive Supplemental Security Income or that adult services are eligibility-based.*

Figure 1, continued

> **Mistake #10: Not Enough Prep Time**
> School and/or parents wait too long to start transition planning and services, which means the student does not have the amount of time needed to adequately remedy transition-related skills deficits.
>
> **Example:** *Bob's school waited until he turned 14 to start discussing transition and found that he had significant skill deficits that would take much longer than 4 years to address.*

Note. Adapted from "Top Ten Mistakes to Avoid During Post-Secondary Transition Planning/Evaluation" [Unpublished whitepaper], by J. Williams & B. Bloom, n.d., Council of Parent Advocates and Attorneys. Adapted with permission of the authors.

options after high school, including college. It is the responsibility of students, parents, teachers, and other educational professionals to provide the information and support to make college a reality.

IEP Process

As you begin to consider your future plans, it is essential that you become an active part of your Individualized Education Program (IEP). According to IDEA (2004), a statement of needed transition services that includes strategies and activities that will assist the student in preparing for postsecondary activities must be included in the IEP at least by the time the child turns 16 years of age, and it must be updated annually. The IEP must include:

> (aa) appropriate measurable postsecondary goals based upon age appropriate transition assessments related to training, education, employment and, where appropriate, independent living skills;
> (bb) the transition services (including courses of study) needed to assist the child in reaching those goals; and

(cc) beginning not later than 1 year before the child reaches the age of majority under State law, a statement that the child has been informed of the child's rights under [IDEA], if any, that will transfer to the child on reaching the age of majority. . . . (IDEA, 2004, Section 1414)

More specifically, according to IDEA (2004),

(a) Transition services means a coordinated set of activities for a child with a disability that—
  (1) Is designed to be within a results-oriented process, that is focused on improving the academic and functional achievement of the child with a disability to facilitate the child's movement from school to post-school activities, including postsecondary education, vocational education, integrated employment (including supported employment), continuing and adult education, adult services, independent living, or community participation;
  (2) Is based on the individual child's needs, taking into account the child's strengths, preferences, and interests; and includes—
    (i) Instruction;
    (ii) Related services;
    (iii) Community experiences;
    (iv) The development of employment and other post-school adult living objectives; and
    (v) If appropriate, acquisition of daily living skills and provision of a functional vocational evaluation.
(b) Transition services for children with disabilities may be special education, if provided as specially designed instruction, or a related service, if required to

assist a child with a disability to benefit from special education. (Section 300.43 Transition Services)

Throughout the book we also refer to the *age of majority*: "In many states, individuals assume the rights of adults upon reaching the so-called 'age of majority.' In most jurisdictions, the age of majority is 18 years" (HEATH Resource Center at the National Youth Transitions Center, 2006, p. 34). According to Learning Disabilities Association of America (2013),

> IDEA 2004 requires that at least one year before the student reaches the "age of majority" and legally becomes an adult, the school must (1) alert the student of their new, upcoming responsibilities, and (2) provide notices of upcoming meetings to the student as well as the parents, while all other notices will go only to the student. States determine what the "age of majority" is, so it can vary from state to state. But when the student reaches that age, he or she will assume legal control over educational placement, educational records, eligibility, evaluations and programming, and any mediation or due process needed to resolve disputes. (p. 1)

Certainly, the expansion of the federal law has required educators to be actively involved in addressing future goals and outcomes for students with disabilities. But what does this look like in the school setting?

Learning to Ask the Right Questions

1. Did the transition assessment in which you participated include an assessment related to postsecondary education?

Learning to Ask the Right Questions, continued

2. Does your current IEP include appropriate measurable postsecondary goals?
3. Does your current IEP include a statement of transition services needed to meet the postsecondary goals?
4. Have you been informed that your rights under IDEA will be transferred from your parents to you upon reaching the age of majority (which is typically 18 years of age, but can differ between states)?
5. What role do you have in developing your own transition plan?

Student-Led IEP Meetings

First of all, students must be an active part of the IEP process as soon as possible. This is a judgment call that has to be made by your parents, teachers, and other school staff who are working with you on a regular basis. During your elementary years, you were probably not in attendance at the IEP meeting, but as you become older, your role in the IEP meeting should move to that of an active participant. If this is not the case in your school, you should contact your special education department or the special education case manager to make arrangements for your inclusion in these meetings. If you are a student served under 504, you should contact the Section 504 representative at the school or district to participate in a student-led 504 meeting.

Teachers often report that students who have input on what their goals will be are much more invested in working toward achieving them. Much research has been done to support this evidenced-based practice. Students frequently have something very specific they want to work on, and if given the opportunity, teachers can assist them in figuring out a way to meet those goals. Ownership often breeds success!

Students who have reached the age of majority in their state cannot be denied access to their IEP unless their parents have guardianship. Even so, all students in high school should be included in their IEPs and allowed to give input on goals and objectives for success. In fact, at age 16, you are required by law to be invited, and it is part of the federal accountability system, State Performance Plan Indicator 13, in all states. Transition goals are drafted by the student with the help of other individuals, such as a teacher, parent, or Employment Transition Representative (ETR) prior to the IEP meeting. Sometimes student advocates and/or other service providers assist in this process. The IEP team, which includes the student, will review the transition goals during the IEP team meeting.

Once you begin attending your IEP meetings, Mason et al. (2004) suggested three general levels for your participation, ranging from presenting limited information to assuming responsibility for all aspects of the IEP meeting:

> **Level 1:** Teachers and administrators lead the IEP meeting, but you read or present information about your transition plan. In other words, you talk about what you want to do after high school and what steps you need to take while in high school to reach those goals.

> **Level 2:** Teachers and administrators lead most of the meeting, but you explain your disability and how it affects your school performance, talk about your strengths and weaknesses, and explain the accommodations you need and prefer for success in the classroom.

> **Level 3:** At this level, you lead the entire IEP meeting. Although it initially may be easier for teachers and administrators to lead the IEP meeting, the benefits for you to take on this role can be significant. Leading the meeting gives you an opportunity to advocate for yourself, develop your professional communication skills, and build your self-confidence. Specific IEP meeting instructions vary from school to school, and your teachers will be able to teach you this process as you become more involved and independent in participating in your IEP meeting.

Providing Student Support

Without specific IEP meeting instructions, students may not know what to do, may not understand the purpose of the meeting or what is being said, and may feel as if no one is interested in what they have to say (Martin et al., 2006). Learning to lead the IEP meeting gives you more ownership in developing your transition plan and encourages you to focus on future goals. The following are some of the steps involved in learning to become an active part of the actual process:

> - Learn the IEP process and the components of the IEP.
> - Learn about your disability and how it affects you academically and physically.
> - Study your current IEP and meet with the assessment team to gain a better understanding of assessment results and how the results apply to your disability.
> - Meet with the teacher and parents to develop a draft of your IEP. This pre-IEP meeting will give you an opportunity to communicate your goals and objectives.

As you begin learning about the IEP process, the range of your involvement in the IEP meeting should increase. Eventually, you may be able to lead the entire meeting. Research shows that students who lead their IEP meetings increase their confidence, communication skills, leadership skills, and advocacy skills (Mason et al., 2004). These skills will provide lasting benefits for students who are pursuing a postsecondary education.

Learning to Ask the Right Questions

1. What role do you have in your IEP meetings?
2. Do you understand the goals that are written on your IEP?
3. Do you understand the accommodations that are written on your IEP?

Transition Timelines

In 2009, a number of states began working together to develop rigorous standards in English language arts and mathematics that build toward college and career readiness by the time students graduate from high school (U.S. Department of Education, n.d.-a). The federal government has supported this state-led effort, and most states have adopted the standards. These College- and Career-Ready Standards build from kindergarten through 12th grade to support students' preparation and success upon graduation. The college and career readiness skills that each student needs are directly tied to their individual postsecondary goals for college and career.

As stated in IDEA (2004), your IEP will need to include a statement of transition services as defined earlier in this chapter. This statement will be based upon your needs while taking into account your preferences and interests. It will include:

> - instruction,
> - related services,
> - community experiences,
> - employment,
> - independent living,
> - acquisition of daily living skills (when needed), and
> - functional vocational evaluation (when needed).

Transition plan development may involve a number of people to ensure that all areas of the plan are addressed. You and your family, special education teacher, guidance counselor, vocational educator, therapists, adult agency service providers, and others who may be needed to plan for a smooth transition may be invited to participate.

Again, the transition services must be based on your needs, preferences, and interests as a student to successfully meet the postsecondary outcomes. Academic decisions related to the required coursework will need to begin in the middle school years. You will want to make sure you are taking the courses that will fulfill the requirements of a postsecondary institution. The following sections provide information at each grade level to be used in the planning process, including checklists for your use. In addition, the Appendix includes frequently asked questions regarding postsecondary education and students with disabilities.

Eighth Grade

For students who are planning for college, if you have not already begun to discuss transition services, eighth grade is the year to discuss transition into high school with parents, the IEP team, and the guidance counselor. You will need to develop a master plan that will include the courses you will need for high school graduation and those you might need in order to attend community or 4-year colleges. Here are some actions you will want to take during your eighth-grade year:

> ➤ Obtain a copy of the high school course of study catalogue, or if this is not available, a listing of diploma requirements from the school counselor. Most schools will be able to provide you with an alignment of diploma requirements to College- and Career-Ready Standards.
> ➤ Review the websites of possible postsecondary colleges you may be interested in so that you can become familiar with the course requirements for acceptance, as well as any entrance exams that may be required.
> ➤ Develop the high school course of study plan based on the requirements of the colleges in which you are interested.
> ➤ Some colleges may recommend or require additional courses. For instance, if you are interested in attending an art school,

you may need to add 4 years of art study to this slate of general coursework.

> If you do not already have a transition plan as part of your IEP, you and your parents should arrange to have it included at this time. You have the legal right to request it be included prior to age 16 (the age at which federal law dictates that a transition statement must be included). Many students will start this discussion earlier.

> You may want to take an extra study skills course or summer program to help you begin expanding your techniques and learning how technology can be used to assist in studying.

> Start saving money. Your parents can start looking into various savings plans for your education. You also might consider entering contests, which often include scholarships, cash prizes, and savings bonds as awards. Saving personal money now can help you slowly put aside spending money for college.

> Remediate and/or compensate for basic skill deficits through tutoring or summer coursework. Consider improving your skills relating to technology use while you are in middle school and high school. Use the opportunity to learn to become proficient and independent in order to more easily participate in college-level online classes or in the event the college moves to online-only classes as a result of a natural disaster or pandemic. For example, this happened in some institutions during Hurricane Harvey, the California wildfires, and the COVID-19 pandemic.

You will want to determine the best method to organize the documents you accumulate throughout the high school years that will prove helpful to you while planning for college. For example, get a folder or binder to keep your course of study catalogue and other important papers. It is never too soon to start this folder, and it is a great way to keep important information together. If you have any of this information in a digital format, set up a digital folder on your desktop. This will ensure that everything needed for the college application process is located in one place and is easily accessible. Because students with disabilities have an IEP, they are eligible to remain in the public school system through the age of 21. However, if a student ages out during the school year, certain provisions apply. If this is your case, the next section may be extended over the 6–7 years that you remain at the high school level. However, this decision will be made in conjunction with you and your IEP team.

Ninth Grade

This typically is the beginning of the high school years and is the time to start thinking about the possibility of pursuing a postsecondary education. There are certain actions you will need to take each year as you progress through high school so that you are prepared to transition into a college or university. You also may use this information as a guide or checklist to help you remain on track in preparing for life after high school. The following is a list of actions to take during your ninth-grade year of high school:

> Visit the high school career center; typically, it will have a wealth of information and resources available to help you begin looking at colleges and will provide many services for students with disabilities. Your career center counselor or advisor also has multiple career inventories and tests that can help you determine what your future field may be (which can affect the type of postsecondary schooling you will want to pursue).

> Continue developing skills for academic independence, such as time management, study skills, and note-taking. This does not mean you shouldn't utilize available accommodations for these skills, but that you should make sure you begin to develop your own abilities in these areas and recognize your strengths and weaknesses.

> Explore assistive technology tools and make sure you can use computer software programs, including word processing and

spreadsheets. Many of these programs can be used on mobile devices, such as an iPhone or iPad, so make sure you are familiar with those as well. Tutorials for these software programs are available online.

> At the annual IEP meeting, make sure you are taking the required courses for high school graduation. Also, discuss any college entrance exams that might be required with the school counselor. The school counselor will need to complete the necessary paperwork to allow your identified testing accommodations to be used with these entrance exams. Your counselor may also be able to direct you to test prep programs that have worked well for other students in the past.

> Work with your school counselor to set up a plan for taking college entrance exams. These exams can be taken multiple times during your high school years. The PSAT exam also offers practice tests during your 10th- and 11th-grade years. By making a schedule of when you will take these exams, you can be better prepared and make time for studying in advance. However, know that if you are a student with a disability who receives testing accommodations as part of your IEP, you also will qualify for testing accommodations on college exams. To begin this process, visit the Educational Testing Service website at https://www.ets.org/gre/revised_general/register/disabilities for accommodations for test takers with disabilities.

> Explore and choose some of the extracurricular activities you want to become involved in during high school. This important information will be requested on all college applications, so you should keep a file that documents dates and activities in which you participate. Such activities also can lead you to other postsecondary opportunities you may have otherwise overlooked—for example, a drama club or class may spark a talent for acting, pointing you toward a fine arts college.

> Explore options for completing some community service projects. Again, this information will be requested on all college

applications, so a file should be kept that documents dates and activities throughout high school.

➤ Continue to remediate and/or compensate for basic skill deficits.

➤ Work hard in all of your classes, so you can keep up your GPA. Take advantage of teachers who offer extra study sessions or tutorials before and after school, as these may be good opportunities to get one-on-one time with your instructors.

Tenth Grade

Once you have completed your first year of high school, you need to begin thinking about possible postsecondary options. The focus of your 10th-grade year will be much the same as the previous year, but there are some additional actions that you need to pursue during this school year. The following actions should be taken in the 10th-grade year:

➤ Review your 4-year plan and high school transcript with the IEP team and school counselor. At this point, if it is determined that any coursework is missing, you'll want to adjust your schedule or prepare for summer courses.

➤ Sign up for and take a practice college entrance exam.

➤ Remember to check out the Educational Testing Services website (https://www.ets.org) for information on testing accommodations for students with disabilities.

➤ Visit a nearby college and talk with someone who works with students who have disabilities. All campuses should have an office that assists prospective and current students with disabilities. It also may be beneficial to talk with current university students with disabilities to get their advice on college planning.

➤ Continue your involvement in extracurricular activities and community service. This may be a good time to take on leadership roles within those activities by offering to lead projects or work on committees.

> Continue academic preparation and remediation/compensation strategies. Identify any assistive technology needs.
> Continue to work hard in all of your classes, so you can keep up your GPA. Also, keep taking advantage of any one-on-one time with your teachers—a good sophomore year does not mean that you should not continue successful work habits and strategies in the years to come.
> Typically, students conduct their college visits in 11th grade, but because you may be searching for colleges and universities that offer varying levels of support for students with disabilities, it would be best to start researching those types of programs this year.

Eleventh Grade

Many high school counselors refer to the 11th-grade year as the most important year for students pursuing a college education. It is during this year that a large number of students take their college entrance exams. Plus, when students begin completing college applications in the summer prior to their senior year or the fall semester of their senior year, the last full year of grades they have to submit is from their 11th-grade year. Therefore, you want to make sure you have a strong academic year and remain on track as you move closer to graduation. During your 11th-grade year, you should take the following actions:

> Review your 4-year plan and high school transcript with the IEP team and school counselor. Make sure that you are still on track for graduation.
> Sign up for and take a college entrance exam. You also may consider taking a preparatory course for this exam in the semester before you take it, or you can take free practice exams through the College Board website (see https://collegereadiness. collegeboard.org/sat/practice/full-length-practice-tests). You should have already checked out the Educational Testing

Services website (https://www.ets.org) for information on testing accommodations for students with disabilities during the 10th-grade year, but there is still time to do so now if you act quickly.

➤ Attend a college night at your high school or a local college fair to obtain additional information from colleges in which you might be interested.

➤ Visit those college websites in which you are interested in applying to determine which applications are accepted. Common applications used are the Common Application (https://www.commonapp.org), Coalition for College Application (https://www.coalitionforcollegeaccess.org), and the Universal College Application (https://www.universalcollegeapp.com). Other colleges may have college specific applications that they prefer you to use. You may begin completing this application at your convenience.

➤ Identify at least two teachers and two other people you could use as references on your college application. At least one of these persons should be from your community: someone you have worked with in your community service, an employer, or a community leader, such as your religious leader or camp counselor.

➤ Begin visiting colleges you may be interested in attending. Take advantage of special visitation services, such as campus tour guides. Make an appointment to talk with someone who works with students who have disabilities. Make sure to find out what services the college provides for students with disabilities to help determine if the college is a match. Find current students with disabilities from whom you can receive advice and guidance.

➤ Continue your involvement in extracurricular activities and community service. Now is a great time to begin taking on leadership roles (no matter how small they may be). You also should keep in mind that solid participation and leadership in one or two activities can be just as significant on your application, if not more so, than minor membership or participation in multiple activities.

> Continue academic preparation and remediation/compensation strategies, assistive technology use, and self-advocacy skills.
> Begin looking at and applying for scholarships independent from universities. Many exist for students with disabilities who wish to complete a postsecondary education. Resources for financial aid and scholarships can be found in the Resources section at the end of this book.
> Prepare transition packets for disability documentation that include evaluation reports, transcripts, test scores, current IEP, medical records, writing samples, and letters of recommendation. You will want to work with your school counselor and/or administrators and administrative assistants to get official copies of some of these documents.
> Keep working hard in all of your classes, so you can keep up your GPA.

Figure 2 provides a copy of a comprehensive junior year planning checklist developed by college planning expert Sandra Berger (2014). Although this checklist originally was created for use with gifted students, its information has proven to be helpful to all students applying for college. You can review and modify this list with your parents and counselor, perhaps spreading some of its suggested actions across 2 years of school. Keep in mind that there are many lists like this one available. You should always modify such lists to match your needs and goals.

Twelfth Grade

This is not the year to stop working! Senior year is a busy time for students, and it can be difficult to remain focused academically. Even though you may have completed the application process to some col-

Figure 2
Junior Year Planning Checklist

College Planning Portfolio

Who Am I?
____ Consider a summer activity such as:
- ❑ a summer internship;
- ❑ travel;
- ❑ courses offered by talent search programs on a campus (i.e., the opportunity to acquire college credits and try out a college lifestyle); or
- ❑ a college planning seminar (offered by many colleges for a week or more to help you get a headstart on applications and other elements).

Where Am I Going?
____ Create a chart that lists:
- ❑ application deadlines (including early action and early decision dates);
- ❑ financial aid deadlines (they are often different at different colleges);
- ❑ tests required by colleges that interest you;
- ❑ costs including student fees and the other extras;
- ❑ number and type of recommendations required; and
- ❑ interview deadlines and locations.

What Do I Like?
____ Develop a list of 8–10 colleges. Work up a comparison chart. Include factors that are important to you, and keep in mind the following factors:
- ❑ size (campus, number of students);
- ❑ geographic location (urban, rural, North, South, etc.);
- ❑ course offerings (Do they teach what you like?);
- ❑ cost (tuition, room and board, books, travel to and from home, etc.);
- ❑ available scholarships or tuition assistance programs;
- ❑ extracurricular activities (newspaper, sports, etc.);

Figure 2, continued

> ❑ academic advising and career counseling procedures; and
> ❑ student access to required readings, laboratory space, and computer time.
>
> **Some Additional Points to Consider Include:**
> ❑ Email colleges to request information and application forms for 6–10 colleges. If schools prefer that you use online applications, download them. Keep all information so you can avoid typing the same info repeatedly. Copy-paste is easier than retyping.
> ❑ Make appointments for personal interviews at colleges you plan to visit in the fall or winter.
> ❑ Recheck application deadlines. Start filling out application forms early in the fall. Learn how to complete an error-free application. Make extra copies of each application form. Use the copies for practice before completing the originals.
> ❑ Unless instructions say otherwise, type everything. If you can't type, consider using a computerized application. Have someone proofread every word on your application forms. Correct all errors.
> ❑ Make and keep copies of everything.
> ❑ Think about three teachers you might ask to write a recommendation for you. (You might wind up with 1 or 2.) Talk to each one about your favorite activities and academic subject and remind them if you won an award.
> ❑ Your counselor may be asked for a letter of recommendation. List all of your activities and leadership positions. List your academic accomplishments. Don't expect that your counselor will remember your accomplishments if they are responsible for 500+ students.

Note. Adapted from *College Planning for Gifted Students: Choosing and Getting Into the Right College* (Updated ed., pp. 19–21), by S. L. Berger, 2014, Taylor & Francis. Copyright 2014 by Taylor & Francis. Adapted with permission.

leges, the admissions office will request a copy of your final grades upon graduation. Colleges have been known to retract their offer of admission if there has been a significant decrease in your academic performance or extracurricular activities and community service. In your final year of high school, you should take the following actions:

> Review your 4-year plan and high school transcript with the IEP team and school counselor. Has everything been completed so that you can graduate? Compensate for missing coursework by changing your schedule, if needed.

> Sign up for and take a college entrance exam if you are interested in raising your previous scores. Again, you may want to consider preparatory courses, especially if your goal is to raise your scores.

> Visit any colleges that you are still considering applying to, but remember that the deadlines typically occur in the fall of your senior year. If you need to narrow down your choices further, you may want to do last-minute visits to colleges early in the year or during the summer before your senior year.

> In preparation for the college application, work with your English teacher to complete your college essay. You also should schedule time with another teacher or your counselor to proofread your essay.

> Continue your involvement with extracurricular activities and community service. Start thinking about which activities you would like to continue in college.

> Strengthen self-advocacy skills. You can take legal responsibility for your education at the age of 18.

> Apply for scholarships for the following year. Again, take notice of awards geared toward students with disabilities. You and your parents also should work with your school counselor to complete the Free Application for Federal Student Aid (FAFSA), so that you are eligible for grants and student loans. Keep in mind that if you do not fill out a FAFSA, you cannot receive federal aid. Also note that there are federal, state, and college deadlines for submitting the FAFSA. Be sure to review

the dates carefully. If you miss a college deadline, your application may still be accepted later in the year, but it is a first come, first serve system (see https://studentaid.gov/apply-for-aid/fafsa/fafsa-deadlines#federal). Take note that:

> Students with disabilities must document for the financial aid administrator the expenses related to their disabilities that are not provided for by another source. This task again calls for self-confidence and self-advocacy skills that often have not been well developed in secondary school in students with disabilities. Students with disabilities must undertake the difficult and complex task of cataloguing and documenting all of the expenses related to their disabilities and reducing that amount by support received from elsewhere, such as VR. This is a formidable challenge that would test the skills of anyone and is sometimes unreasonable for students with disabilities. (Wolanin & Steele, 2004, p. 59)

- ➤ Continue working hard in all of your classes so you can finish with a strong GPA. This may be more difficult during senior year because you naturally are ready to graduate, but remember to stay focused.
- ➤ Once you receive acceptance, if you've received multiple acceptance letters, talk with your family and visit those schools to make a decision. Then, begin the planning process for attendance, including housing, travel arrangements, academic advising, and other necessities (many of which we will explain later in this book).

This is an exciting time, and there is a great deal of planning that occurs prior to heading off to college. Make sure you keep current, accurate records and that your transition plan is updated annually so you remain on track.

For additional academic support, look into Advancement Via Individual Determination (AVID) at your school. AVID is an elective class in which students who wish to attend college can benefit from the support of daily instruction in order to be successful in a college prep course of study. During the AVID class, tutors work with individual students to assist them in developing higher level thinking and independent study skills (see https://www.avid.org).

Learning to Ask the Right Questions

1. How will you make sure you are following a timeline to achieve your postsecondary goals?
2. Do you have a designated place to keep your course of study catalogue or copy of your 4-year plan, as well as other important papers that you are collecting while you are in high school?
3. Is your IEP updated at each IEP meeting to reflect the current status of your transition goals?
4. Can you clearly explain your disability? Do you have a copy of the documentation identifying you as a student with a disability as well as documentation of the current accommodations you are receiving in high school?

Conclusion

If you are a student with a disability who is considering a college education, the planning process has to begin early. Fortunately, the changes in federal laws over the past decades have given you a greater role and responsibility in planning for your future by making you an integral part of the IEP team and all of the decision-making responsibilities that are afforded the team. Not only will you be actively involved in writing your IEP, but you may also be leading the meeting.

Along with the expanded role you will play in developing your IEP, there are numerous steps involved in preparing for a post-secondary education. Beginning early will help pave the way for a smooth transition from high school to college. With the detailed information organized by grade level in this chapter, you can create a guideline or checklist to aid you in the planning process. In addition, the Appendix shares some frequently asked questions provided by the Eleanor and Charles Garrett Center on Transition and Disability Studies. These questions address what students with disabilities and their families need to know about postsecondary education.

Student Interviews

What steps did you take to begin the transition process during your high school years?

James: The first and most important step I took was to decide that I *wanted* to go to college and become a successful adult. As much as our parents may want us to attend college, as individuals with disabilities, we must have the level of self-determination to make it happen. Both parents and school systems can and should provide us with the appropriate strategies; however, if we are not self-determined, success is difficult, if not impossible, to achieve. Another important step that I took was to begin researching my options both independently and with assistance. In reality, though, most of the assistance came from my parents and from my social coach at FOCUS Initiative, a for-profit organization that provides various services to individuals with autism spectrum disorders. Again, my actions were always driven by my level of self-determination.

Angela: Throughout middle school and high school I had help from my parents, private tutoring, modifications such as fewer answer choices and extra time, and I went to Content Mastery. Once in high school, I saw a tutoring specialist once a week. I took the SAT test but scored too low to get into college, and my grades were not good either. Once it came close to the summer after high school, I realized I needed to do something, and so I attended Houston Community College all summer and completed 13 hours of credit. I transferred into Sam Houston State University (SHSU) and was ready to begin in the fall. No one believed I would ever make it to college or complete college for that matter. They gave me options such as community colleges and told me about looking for a job. I was determined to get into SHSU, and after a long summer of hard work, I finally realized I could be successful, and I was on my way.

Jared: The first step that I took was deciding I wanted to go to college. I then made a list of the colleges that met the criteria that I was looking for. After narrowing the list down, I went and visited college campuses and took various campus tours.

Ricky: I knew I wanted to go to college, and because I have two older sisters who had already gone through the college application process, my parents and I knew about the steps I would need to take. When I took my PSATs I did not score very well, so I took a private SAT prep class. I was able to get accommodations such as unlimited time, which helped because I typically had anxiety about test taking. I had already visited a lot of colleges because my dad was a high school football coach and had athletes who were recruited and played for some major colleges. That brought exposure to college at a young age.

What resources did you find most helpful in making plans to attend college?

James: There is so much good information on the Internet regarding colleges, degrees, and career paths. I did have to know where to start, and for that information I asked my brother, who was already in college, and my counselor's office. There was a lot of good information available through my local library, as well, and I found it to be a good place to dig in and get information. I also found good information through some of my local state agencies, although the information was hard to find and sometimes confusing. Honestly, this part of my transition was probably the most difficult due to the fact that there were very few places you could find an organized batch of information. Because of this, I started a transition resource website a while back called Transition Matters that provides documents and links to information regarding postsecondary transition for students with Asperger's syndrome or high-functioning autism. The content of this site has since been moved to a resource page on my current employer's website (https://www.bloomconsultingco.com/weblinks). This page consolidates many of the resources I have found helpful in addressing my own transition needs.

Angela: I had two older sisters who had both attended 4-year colleges, and I had been aware of the process by watching them go through it. My older sister is dyslexic. I watched how hard she worked and saw that she succeeded. She had found that the teachers at SHSU would work with her and were more personable, unlike another university from which she had transferred. I also made a lot of phone calls myself to seek additional information. The calls I made were mainly to the student center at the university. My parents also were very supportive and always kept the standards high for me. They believed in me.

Jared: The resource that was most helpful to me was the counselor's office at my high school. I was able to meet with the counselor to discuss my options and goals. I also accessed the Internet to find additional information and seek answers to my questions.

Ricky: I used some of the resources and advice from the guidance department at school as well as my parents' advice.

What are your recommendations on finding a college that can address a student's specific needs?

James: First, I would develop a plan that includes my future goals. Then I would take those goals and use them as a starting point. Although the design may vary by state, I would hope that most high school transition plans would include these goals and steps to achieve them. The key point to remember, though, is that IDEA only requires a plan to be written when the student reaches the age of 16, and many students would greatly benefit from an informal plan being written at an earlier age. For example, I wanted to become a teacher in special education and go to a school within 3 hours of my parents' home. So, I compiled a list of all of the schools that offered that degree. Then, I went to the university websites and began narrowing my choices. I contacted both the Services for Students With Disabilities Coordinator and the College of Education Dean's Office to learn more about what they offered. Based on that information, I scheduled personal visits. A strong indicator that you have found a supportive environment is the culture or attitude of the campus. The term *culture* is used to describe the willingness of an institution to provide accommodations to students with disabilities, as well as the quality of those accommodations. An institution with a good culture would be one that educates its faculty and staff about disabilities, provides services that exceed the minimum required, and strives to welcome and actively recruit students with disabilities to its campus. For example, a college can be grounded in tradition, but still be progressive and proactive in its effort to assist and promote the attendance of individuals with disabilities.

Angela: Talk to people who already attend the colleges and make college visits. Make a list of questions and answer them for each prospective college, as well as a pro and con list for each school.

Jared: I believe you need to look for what you want in a college, including the size of the college or university. Also, does it have the major you are looking for, and will you be comfortable living and going to school there?

Ricky: I tried to network with other students I knew who had the same academic struggles I did, as well as talking to older kids I knew who were already in college. I did not find that college websites were very informative about their programs for students with LD. It didn't occur to me to ask about these specific accommodations, but I think now I would go directly to check out how a college of interest could support LD.

2

Stand Up for Yourself

Advocacy

Knowing Your Rights and Responsibilities

As the number of students with disabilities who are entering and graduating from postsecondary institutions continues to increase (Joshi & Bouck, 2017), these students must know what services are available as well as the process to access these services. Understanding the law is a critical component in planning for a smooth transition into a postsecondary institution. Without this information, you may not receive all of the services that the educational system—both secondary and postsecondary institutions—is required to provide. Students, parents, and educators of students with disabilities have to be knowledgeable and proactive in making sure that information is accessible and accurate. Keeping current on changes within the state

 DOI: 10.4324/9781003233749-3

and federal laws may have a significant impact on the information that is included in your transition plan.

Federal Laws: IDEA, ADA, and Section 504

While in the public school system, students with disabilities are provided services based on the Individuals With Disabilities Education Act (IDEA, 2004). Under IDEA, school districts are required to provide a free appropriate education to students with disabilities based on their individualized educational needs. The services may include an educational setting within a continuum of special education placements and accommodations and modifications to the regular education program, including adjustments in test-taking procedures, assignments, and grading, as well as related services, such as physical therapy (Gil, 2007).

Students not covered under IDEA may be covered under Section 504 of the Rehabilitation Act of 1973 and the Americans With Disabilities Act (ADA) of 1990. Section 504 and ADA are civil rights laws that provide equal access and opportunity and prevent discrimination. However, once a student completes the 12th grade, IDEA is no longer applicable in the educational setting; therefore, services for students with disabilities in postsecondary institutions are provided under Section 504 and ADA. In most cases, postsecondary disability service providers interpret Section 504 and ADA guidelines to mean that a specific diagnosis with a clearly established functional limitation in a major life activity is required (National Joint Committee on Learning Disabilities, 2007).

Public colleges and universities generally receive federal financial assistance. There are some private colleges and universities that do not receive any federal assistance; therefore, Section 504 does not apply to them. When you are researching private postsecondary institutions, be sure to inquire whether or not they receive federal assistance.

Table 1 provides a comparison of the rights and responsibilities between secondary and postsecondary education for students with disabilities. In addition, a resource from the U.S. Department of Education's Office for Civil Rights (2011a), "Students With Disabilities Preparing for Postsecondary Education: Know Your Rights and Responsibilities," can assist you in identifying important issues as you make the transition from high school to college (see https://www2.ed.gov/about/offices/list/ocr/transition.html).

As is evident in Table 1, changes in the rights and responsibilities you will be expected to carry out when moving from high school to a postsecondary institution are significant. The responsibility shifts from the school to the student. Therefore, as a college-bound student, you need to have a repertoire of specific skills that will prepare you to take on such responsibility and overcome transition challenges.

Family Education Rights and Privacy Act

Student records are private and are protected by the Family Educational Rights and Privacy Act (FERPA), which was established in 1974 to protect the confidentiality of student medical and disability records. Disability records typically are kept by the university disabilities office. Files often are secured with access limited to appropriate personnel. FERPA protects you by not allowing your records to be shared with any party without your consent. This includes the faculty, your parents, administrators, and public entities such as the press.

Table 1

The Rights and Responsibilities of Students With Disabilities in Secondary and Postsecondary Education

Secondary Education	Postsecondary Education
Students Are Protected by: » IDEA » Section 504 » ADA	Students Are Protected by: » Section 504 » ADA
Responsibilities for Identification and Evaluation: » The school district is responsible for the identification and evaluation at the district's expense.	Responsibilities for Identification and Evaluation: » Students must self-identify and provide documentation of a disability at their own cost.
Service Delivery: » School districts are responsible for providing special education programs and services as identified in the student's IEP. The IEP team will decide on issues of placement, accommodations, or modifications, and it may be necessary to alter a program or curriculum in order for the student to be successful. » School districts must provide personal services when noted in the student's IEP, including assistive technology, transportation, and personal attendants.	Service Delivery: » Students are responsible for notifying the Student Disability Services Office staff of their disability to discuss reasonable accommodations. Accommodations are provided in order for students with disabilities to have equal access to all programs and activities, but the essential program requirements are not altered. » Postsecondary institutions are not responsible for providing any services that are not available to all students.

Table 1, continued

Secondary Education	Postsecondary Education
Enforcing the Law: » The IEP team or the school professional in charge of the student's 504 plan is required to oversee the implementation of the student's services. » IDEA is enforced by the Office of Special Education and Rehabilitative Services in the U.S. Department of Education, while Section 504 and ADA are civil rights statues overseen by the Office of Civil Rights and the U.S. Department of Justice in conjunction with the Equal Employment Opportunity Commission (EEOC).	Enforcing the Law: » The student is responsible for asking the Disability Support Services staff to provide letters notifying professors of approved accommodations. » Section 504 and ADA are civil rights statues overseen by the Office of Civil Rights and the U.S. Department of Justice in conjunction with the Equal Employment Opportunity Commission (EEOC).
Advocacy: » Parents or guardians are the primary advocates for a student's needs.	Advocacy: » Students must advocate for their own academic needs and services.

Learning to Ask the Right Questions

1. Do you have a basic understanding of your rights and responsibilities as a student with disabilities in high school?
2. Do you have a basic understanding of how your rights and responsibilities as a student with disabilities change after you complete high school and move into a college or university setting?
3. Do you know where to find answers to questions you might have regarding your rights and responsibilities as a student with disabilities?

Advocacy in Action

Clearly, there are a number of skills that students with disabilities need for a successful transition. The foundation for these skills needs to be formed during the middle and high school years. Once a student leaves the public school and moves into an institution of higher education, they must advocate for their own academic needs and services. Therefore, at this transition point, as the student, you need to be able to make decisions and determine the path of your college career. Legally, colleges and universities cannot share pertinent information regarding your academic progress to your parents unless a release of information authorizing your parents to access this material is secured. Nevertheless, you will need to advocate for yourself.

Self-advocacy can be defined as "the ability to act on what the individual knows about his or her needs, even though people may not offer the individual a clear choice or ask the individual to state his or her needs" (Van-Belle et al., 2006, p. 40). The importance of teaching or helping individuals to realize the need to self-advocate is of growing concern. More and more students with disabilities are entering the college setting with little or no skills in the area of self-advocacy. Most students are not taught these skills during their high school years and do not realize the need to obtain self-advocacy skills.

When students enter the college setting, they move from a system designed to include a large degree of parental involvement (in other words, the student's disability is managed by someone else) to one built on student independence. For example, in high school, parents attend the IEP meeting, and the IEP team determines objectives and accommodations, but in college, you must determine and ensure that you receive accommodations. The change to being responsible for your education might seem overwhelming to you, but you are not alone:

> Unfortunately, the autonomy that the Family Education Rights and Privacy Act promotes is a shock to

many students. Add to this surprise the reality that the major tenets of disability legislation for higher education (Section 504 of the Rehabilitation Act and the Americans with Disabilities Act) call for equal access, not guaranteed academic success, and it is no wonder that many students find the task of self-advocacy overwhelming. (McCarthy, 2007, p. 12)

In part, that is why books such as this one can be so important to your college career. We recommend that all students with disabilities seek out local programs offered through universities that specifically address self-advocacy skills. Many programs will target the skills necessary to successfully advocate for oneself at the college level. Essential components of an effective self-advocacy skills program include:

> Keep it simple. Know your disability and how it affects your learning.
> Learn your legal rights under IDEA, Section 504, and ADA.
> Determine reasonable accommodations directly related to your disability.
> Become more independent.
> Create effective study patterns.
> Manage your time.
> Practice and role-play effective self-advocacy skills.

If you are unable to attend specific workshops geared toward self-advocacy skills, you can begin to develop self-advocacy skills by taking responsibility for your actions. It is recommended that students understand their disability and how it affects them, their learning style, and their strengths and weaknesses, and develop study skills and compensatory strategies (Gil, 2007). The following is a list of information that you will need to be able to communicate to those who are a part of your educational program. You need to be able to:

> explain the disability and your specific needs, and practice sharing this information with your teachers and parents;
> identify your areas of strengths and needs, both academic and physical (e.g., Do you have good computer skills? Do you have strong verbal skills? Are you a good athlete?);
> request needed accommodations and discuss changes that need to be made with your school's disabilities coordinator or counselor if these accommodations are not working;
> explain your legal rights and responsibilities (in some college classes, you may be more informed than your instructor regarding the laws that apply to students with disabilities in the academic setting, and, therefore, you need to be well-informed and have accurate legal information);
> schedule meetings with your professors to discuss accommodations and academic progress (remember, professors prefer to hear from students *before* they are failing the class); and
> realize that you are responsible for your life choices.

Your high school teachers may recommend some steps to take to in order to better prepare you with the skills you need to succeed in postsecondary education. These may include:
> helping you understand your disability,
> accepting responsibility for your own success,
> taking pre-preparatory curriculum,
> learning time management skills,
> acquiring computer skills,
> considering supplemental postsecondary programs,
> researching postsecondary programs, and
> getting involved on campus (U.S. Department of Education, 2011b).

Self-Determination

> Self determination is believing you can control your own destiny. Self-determination is a combination of attitudes and abilities that lead people to set goals for themselves, and to take the initiative to reach these goals. It is about being in charge, but is not necessarily the same thing as self-sufficiency or independence. It means making your own choices, learning to effectively solve problems, and taking control and responsibility for one's life. Practicing self-determination also means one experiences the consequences of making choices. (PACER's National Parent Center on Transition and Employment, n.d., para. 1)

Basically, self-determination emphasizes the development of skills and attitudes that enable individuals to become change agents in their own lives, making wise choices that increase the likelihood of achieving their desired goals (Field et al., 2003). People who are self-determined tend to make things happen. They set goals and pursue them: "Self determination enables individuals to take responsibility for their lives by defining and accomplishing goals" (Bashir et al., 2000, p. 52).

Research shows that self-determination may play a role in improving student outcomes, including academic performance, employment, postsecondary participation, and independence (Field et al., 2003; Martin et al., 2003; Wehmeyer & Palmer, 2003). As a result, promoting students' self-determination has become an important component of best practices in the education of students with disabilities.

As you enter into the college setting, you must have a clear understanding of your own limitations, needs, and abilities. This understanding will provide the basis for the development of self-determination. Wehmeyer (2002) identified seven components in which educators can promote student self-determination, which you can use to help you develop this skill. These include:

> setting personal goals,
> solving problems that act as barriers to achieving these goals,
> making appropriate choices based on personal preferences and interests,
> participating in decisions that impact the quality of your life,
> advocating for yourself,
> creating action plans to achieve goals, and
> self-regulating and self-managing day-to-day actions.

As you begin to take a more active role in your educational program and transition planning, you must have the opportunity to practice with some of your teachers while you are still attending public school. This practice is important because:

> unfortunately, all too often students with disabilities enter postsecondary programs lacking understanding of how their disability affects their learning. As a result they are unable to effectively articulate the services and supports needed to meet the academic challenges in college. (Getzel & Thoma, 2008, p. 83)

In order to assist you with this task, use the Self-Advocacy Skills Worksheet at the end of this chapter to help you identify and discuss your educational needs.

Staying in College

Who are the students who complete their college education? In an examination of previous research, students with LD were found to have lower rates of postsecondary completion than their peers without LD despite the existence of policies that focused on ensuring equitable opportunities for students with disabilities at the postsecondary level (Lightfoot et al., 2018). In 2017, the National Center for Learning Disabilities indicated that the rate of college completion for students with LD was 41% compared to 52% of the general student population (Horowitz et al., 2017).

We are not suggesting that students with disabilities cannot be successful in postsecondary education, but that students' decisions about whether or not to pursue a college education depends on their life goals. There also is the reality that some colleges are more "student friendly" than others (Sitlington et al., 2009). More information on knowing which colleges tend to work more collaboratively with students with disabilities can be found in Chapter 4.

Furthermore, research also has shown that there are certain characteristics that tend to be found in students who are successful in college, including students with disabilities. A review conducted by Lightfoot and colleagues (2018) examined intrinsic factors that affected postsecondary academic success. The study found that, for students, a strong drive to succeed, a positive attitude toward themselves and learning, and a belief in their ability to overcome adversity were key factors. Further, the students viewed themselves as being equal to the challenge of college and possessed a strong motivation to succeed.

For students with specific disabilities, immaturity may be a factor, and it may be better to postpone school for a year or two to allow some time to mature and gain some life experience. For example, a characteristic of ADHD is immaturity, which may impact a student's decision to enter college immediately after the completion of high school or delay admittance. Again, this is a personal decision that needs to be made based on input from the IEP team, which hopefully includes the student.

Many students with disabilities have successfully completed a college education and made some excellent career choices. With a willingness to work hard, remain focused, understand your own learning style, and advocate for your needs, you can be one of those successful students. Remember, you are the key to your success!

Learning to Ask the Right Questions

1. Do you understand your disability and how it affects you in the classroom?
2. Can you identify your academic strengths and weaknesses?
3. Do you know your learning style and what accommodations you need for academic success?
4. Do you know what strategies work the best for you in completing academic work?
5. Are you able to communicate your academic needs to your teachers, parents, and fellow students?

Conclusion

As a student with a disability, understanding the law is a critical component in making sure that the laws regarding transition planning are being implemented within your IEP. Reading and understanding the information in Table 1 that identifies the differences in the rights and responsibilities between secondary and postsecondary schools will provide you with a clear overview of what you should expect from your IEP team and the school in regard to your educational planning process.

Beyond the level of understanding comes the responsibility of self-advocating. With your increased involvement in understanding and participating in your transition plan, you will need to know how to explain your disability, identify and express your strengths and areas of need, discuss your accommodations with your teachers and professors, and know what and how to address those in authority when questions arise regarding your academic program. Keeping current on the state and federal laws and how they impact you as a student with a disability will prepare you to advocate for yourself and ensure that your program is designed and implemented according to the law.

Student Interviews

Angela: Yes, I attended and dreaded every moment of them. I hated that everyone involved would talk about me as if I were not sitting there. Some teachers would even use this time to inform my parents of things I had not completed or did poorly on. My role was to sit there and listen to them discuss me. I was asked over and over if I had any questions and helped to determine if there were any other accommodations that I thought would be useful. Then, at the end, they would ask me if what had been decided was okay with me, and I would give my signature.

Jared: When I was in high school it was determined that my disability could be met with a 504 plan instead of an IEP. I was not part of the decision, but my parents were involved in the meetings and decisions.

Ricky: Yes, I attended all my IEP meetings in high school. My parents were also always there with me. Most teachers were very understanding and supportive and always asked me my thoughts and made sure my suggestions and accommodations would work for me. I was very comfortable speaking up regarding my needs and classroom struggles—especially regarding reading and test taking.

Angela: No, not much at all, but my mom was. I felt that my parents as well as teachers sheltered me from my disability, and so there was not a whole lot of information given to me besides what I needed to

49

know to get the help needed on my work. To be honest, though, I wasn't really interested in knowing what was wrong with me either. It just seemed like everything was so hard.

Jared: I was not knowledgeable about any of the laws regarding my rights as a student with a disability. I had to research in order to learn more information to help me navigate the process.

Ricky: I knew that I was protected under the 504 plan and that I could get special assistance in the classroom, but as a high school student I didn't know more than that . . . I just knew I needed some extra support.

How much information did you know regarding your rights and responsibilities as a student with a disability entering a postsecondary institution?

James: At first, I wasn't sure of my rights because most of my knowledge was about IDEA, and my school did little, if anything, to keep me informed of my rights under ADA or Section 504 of the Rehabilitation Act. Although I understand this is due in part to the relative infancy of college transition, I feel we should do much more to educate students with disabilities prior to their arrival on a college campus. I did not begin to fully understand my rights until my freshman year [of college], when I encountered a situation regarding my accommodations. Because of my training in becoming a special educator, I knew where to start looking, and I found most of my answers through the U.S. Department of Education's Office for Civil Rights. However, if I did not have my background in education, I would have had no idea where to start or what to do. The best way to remedy this is to use the point in an IEP meeting when rights are transferred to an adult student to discuss the protections that will be offered to the student in college. Even a self-determined student will find it hard to defend and understand their rights in higher education without significant assistance from parents, educators, or advocates. With that in mind, this process should begin as early as possible with significant emphasis placed on practice of your self-advocacy.

Angela: At first I only went to the disability office because my mom insisted that I go and get help. She left me with no choice. Once I went and started the process of getting accommodations, I became most interested in my learning disabilities. I finally realized that college was going to be extremely hard, and I knew I had to prove to people and myself that I could complete the college coursework. I wouldn't say that I knew much more than [I did in] high school about my rights and responsibilities for college, but I learned a lot going through the process of testing for my disability and setting up my accommodations through the university.

Jared: I was not knowledgeable about any of the rights I had as a student with a disability except knowing I was given extra time to take tests or quizzes.

Ricky: I really did not know much about my rights and responsibilities regarding postsecondary education. I knew that in high school I could be accommodated, but I didn't think these could extend beyond K–12 education.

Did your knowledge of your rights and responsibilities affect your decision in choosing a college?

James: In some ways, this knowledge did affect my ability to choose a college. I purposely tried to choose campuses that seemed open to students with disabilities and up front about our rights. In other words, they viewed their provision of accommodations as a positive and mutually beneficial practice, rather than an obligation mandated under federal law. Although all schools must offer basic accommodations as recipients of federal financial aid, many choose to offer more extensive accommodations and special services in an attempt to attract students with disabilities, which further diversifies their campus and provides equal access to their programs.

Jared: The lack of knowledge that I had did not affect my choice of the college I chose to attend.

Ricky: I was not aware that colleges had to offer any sort of accommodations to students with LD. I thought I'd be on my own to either get help or hire tutors.

What are your recommendations on knowing your rights and responsibilities?

James: The first and most important step in understanding your rights and responsibilities is to read about the basic ideas behind both ADA and Section 504. The laws are confusing and wordy, but several agencies, including the Department of Education's Office for Civil Rights, provide simplified pamphlets and resources on the main ideas. Using that knowledge, brainstorm a list of reasonable accommodations that you believe would enable you to successfully complete the courses your degree requires. Use this knowledge to request accommodations and assistance from your college. If your school's Student Disability Services Office approves certain accommodations, and one of your instructors/professors refuses or seems unwilling to provide them, self-advocate your needs with that professor and handle it in a polite and professional manner. If there is no progress, then it is important that you contact the office and explain the situation. When you do this, keep two things in mind: Approved accommodations are legally protected/enforceable, and you are never required to share your diagnosis with a professor or anyone else if you do not wish to. You are required to disclose your disability to your Student Disability Services Office if you wish to have accommodations, but you don't have to defend or explain your disability to anyone who refuses to provide those accommodations.

Jared: I recommend that anyone who will be attending college with special needs understand your 504 plan or IEP and research the rights you will be given in college.

Ricky: I would go to guidance counselors and case managers because they would know about rights and responsibilities. Then, I would specifically communicate with colleges to see what they offer in the way of support and accommodations.

How did you know that you would have to seek out additional support at college if you struggled with the curriculum (e.g., utilize tutoring through an Academic Success or Academic Resource Center)?

Angela: During my senior year of high school, my teachers made it clear that if I were to want further help after high school then I would have to seek it on my own. Once I got to college, I did a lot of searching myself until I found where I needed to go and what I needed to do.

Jared: It was during my final year in high school that my counselor informed me that if there were times when I needed help in college that I would need to go and seek help by myself. She let me know that no one would be helping me in college. I would have to do it on my own and have to seek out help, and the Academic Resource Center would assist me.

Ricky: I attended Marshall University, and they have a specific program in their school called H.E.L.P., which stands for Higher Education for Learning Problems. It's a nonprofit fee-based program on campus that supports LD students with tutors and mentors. In order to get into this program I had to be interviewed, so once I was accepted into their college I knew it was a requirement.

Self-Advocacy Skills Worksheet

Hi. I'm _____, and I am a student with _____

              (name)

_____ .

That means: _____

_____

_____

_____

My academic strengths are: _____

_____

_____

_____

My areas of academic need are: _____

_____

_____

_____

Some accommodations I need for the classroom are: _____

_____

_____

_____

As a student with a disability, I am provided services under IDEA, Section 504, and ADA. IDEA is a federal law that grants rights to students with disabilities in the public school setting. IDEA will not apply once I am in college. However, Section 504 and ADA are civil rights laws that provide equal access and opportunity, and prevent discrimination, and they do apply when I am in college.

3
College as the Next Step

The journey after high school brings many challenges for students with and without disabilities. Student with disabilities are often faced with higher levels of uncertainty, especially when determining whether or not postsecondary education is a realistic and attainable goal. The decision should not be one that is made in haste, but rather made after careful consideration. Parents often ask whether or not their children should attend college. Unfortunately, the answer to the question cannot be given without carefully analyzing the particular strengths and areas of need that each student has. Comparing students' abilities to the expectations of selected colleges should be a critical factor in the decision-making process. Students with LD should consider the entire continuum of postsecondary education, including 2- and 4-year colleges, vocational/technical schools, GED programs, and adult education programs (Joshi & Bouck, 2017).

Students who decide to postpone college should consider looking into vocational training programs that may offer insight into their

 DOI: 10.4324/9781003233749-4

course of study and give them a head start in the college curriculum. For example, if you want to be a nurse, consider a Certified Nursing Assistant (CNA) program. The Workforce Innovation and Opportunity Act (WIOA) provides a one-time funding opportunity for students ages 14–24 and will pay for certifications in a number of occupations (see https://www.dol.gov/agencies/eta/youth/wioa-formula).

Community College Options

Many students and families seek clarification of differences between 2- and 4-year postsecondary institutions. Many students with disabilities attend community college for their first or only post-secondary education experience (Joshi & Bouck, 2017). Community colleges typically offer programs leading to the acquisition of a 2-year associate degree. However, recent legislation has afforded community colleges the ability to begin offering bachelor's degrees. In addition, postsecondary certificate programs are often offered at the community college level. Many 4-year institutions have developed college transfer agreements with local community colleges. These agreements provide a basic listing of transferable courses offered at the community college level and specify the corresponding 4-year university course for which it will substitute. If you intend to transfer coursework to a 4-year institution, you should meet with an advisor at the community college prior to taking coursework to determine which courses would be considered college transfer courses at the 4-year institution you plan to attend.

Community colleges as an option for students provide lower tuition and fees, the opportunity to continue living at home for continued support from family and friends, greater flexibility in scheduling classes, and an opportunity to improve students' transcripts if they plan to transfer to a 4-year college.

However, some students may choose to attend a 4-year college or university starting with the freshman year. Most of these colleges require that students seek a bachelor's degree focusing on a specific area of study or major. Four-year institutions tend to be more expensive than community colleges. Most 4-year institutions also offer specific career option certifications or licensures, such as teaching or social work.

Selecting a College

After making the decision to attend a college or university for postsecondary education, the next obstacle involves the selection of a college that best matches your individual needs. This selection should not be made solely on whether or not the college has a strong Student Disability Services Office, but rather should be inclusive of several other factors. You must examine your needs and preferences in a variety of areas, including academics, social opportunities, and financial needs. A self-needs assessment involves examining critical questions about your level of self-motivation and independence. Sandler (2008) identified six questions to assess self-motivation and independence in students with ADHD that can be adapted to any disability:

1. Did you need support and structure in high school?
2. Do you routinely need help from others to keep you motivated and focused?
3. Do you thrive on individual attention from teachers?
4. Do you prefer to immerse yourself in a subject?
5. Do you need a high-energy environment?
6. Do you have trouble falling asleep?

Considerations of these questions will help guide you in completing the Postsecondary Preference Worksheet found at the end of this chapter. Completion of this worksheet will allow you to identify specific attributes that you desire in a college setting.

Along with an examination of needs and preferences, you should consider the location of the college campus, explore career goals, research college options, examine the school's disability services, visit college campuses, and most importantly, learn to ask the right questions. In progressing through each of these areas, students and parents often lose sight of the fact that college life extends beyond a student's academic needs. Careful planning for and exploring of college opportunities will enable you to pursue not only academic achievement, but also social acceptance and extracurricular participation.

As you make decisions about which colleges to apply to, remember that there are a variety of resources available to help you select a college that best matches your specific needs and desired preferences. Specific sources of information may include speaking with a school counselor, searching current information on the Internet (use specific search words, such as locations you're interested in or types of schools you want, like vocational colleges), college guides obtained from local bookstores, college and universities admission offices, and lastly, the utilization of a specialized private college counselor. The use of a specialized college counselor can be expensive but may be a good investment (Nadeau, 2006). Such a counselor may be beneficial to students who need assistance with the application process, disability management, crisis intervention, and grievance processes. Students who have heavily relied on parents often view the specialized college counselor as an element of their support system.

Location of College Campus

Whether or not the location of the college campus should be a priority in selecting a college will depend on several factors, including financial costs, easy accessibility to current medical providers, your ability to maintain relationships with family and friends within a specific mile radius, and/or access to transportation. Moving away from home can be difficult for all students regardless of whether or not they have a disability. However, some students with specific disabilities may face higher levels of anxiety or may not have the capability to live independently. If you do not feel you have the capability to live independently, it is possible that specific living skills can be identified and addressed prior to the college transition. If you will need a great deal of support from your family, it may be best to explore college campuses that are within a close driving distance to the family home.

If you do not have the capability or financial means to live on a college campus, you should not rule out college attendance. Selecting a college within a convenient distance from your home will enable you to commute to and from campus while still receiving the necessary supports at home. You may want to consider beginning with a community college for a year or two to save money, and then transferring to a 4-year school. In addition, many colleges now offer online programs, which could reduce the cost of attendance as well. According to the National Center for Education Statistics (2019), there were 6,932,074 students enrolled in distance education courses at degree-granting postsecondary institutions in the fall of 2018.

Learning to Ask the Right Questions

1. Do you want to live on the college campus or commute to and from campus?
2. If you choose to live at home, how far is the commute to the college of your choice? Is public transportation available?
3. Is the college located in a small town or larger city? Will this impact your decision to attend?
4. Where are the parking facilities located? If your disability will require you to park in disability parking spaces, where are they located in relation to the building where your program of study is housed? If you have a disability parking permit and the disability spaces are full, where are you authorized to park?

Exploring Career Goals

Once you determine that college should be the next step in your education, you also must examine what you hope to obtain from attending college. It is likely that you are attending postsecondary education in order to seek employment or move forward in career planning. Specifically identifying your long-term goal is an important factor in selecting a college. However, once the decision is made, it is possible that you may change your mind after the first, second, or third year of college. With this in mind, it is still important to recognize the goals that you have for yourself and explore colleges that offer the programming to meet these goals. For example, if you plan to become a graphic designer, it would be important to narrow down colleges and further examine institutions that offer a degree in this area.

Most high school guidance counselors are well versed in career planning processes. High school transition specialists also will address career goals during the transition planning of the IEP meeting (see Chapter 1 for additional information regarding the high school transition planning process). College and career fairs are excellent ways to explore career options. It is not necessary to choose your future career at this point, but it is important to begin thinking about areas in which you might be interested in the future.

Learning to Ask the Right Questions

1. What degree is needed in order to reach the career path that you have selected?
2. Does the college you are investigating offer a program of study that matches your career goals?
3. Are there specific prerequisite high school courses that must be taken to enter into the program of study that matches your career goals?
4. Do your skills and interests match your career goal?

Learning to Ask the Right Questions, continued

5. Will specific disability-related obstacles prevent you from reaching your career goal?

Cost of College Attendance

Many families find themselves negotiating the college selection process based on the specific tuition and expenses of the college. Most private colleges or universities have higher tuition rates. However, for a student with a disability, there are several benefits that can be received from a private university. Private colleges and universities tend to have lower student-to-instructor ratios. Individuals with unique learning needs may benefit greatly from more personal contact with the faculty member teaching the course. Loans, scholarships, grants, and other means of financial aid may assist in making the attendance at a private university or college possible. Of course, smaller public institutions of higher learning will offer similar ratios, typically at a more affordable cost. Financial aid offices are established to assist students in completing applications and determining which form of aid is needed.

Parents often express concern that their children may not be eligible for scholarships or other gifts and awards because of a disability. In many cases, scholarships are linked to academic or athletic performance. However, there is a vast array of scholarships with unique criteria, including ethnicity, religion, extracurricular involvement, and/or community-based involvement. An excellent resource for finding financial aid options is the HEATH Resource Center at the National Youth Transitions Center (https://www.heath.gwu.edu/financial-aid), which specifically addresses financial aid for students with disabilities. *Planning Ahead: Financial Aid for Students With Disabilities* (HEATH Resource Center at the National Youth Transitions Center, 2015) provides an overview of student financial aid and discusses the roles and responsibilities of those who play a significant part in the process of providing aid to students with disabilities. Information on the financial aid application procedure and timelines for students seeking financial aid are included.

For students with disabilities, vocational rehabilitation (VR) agencies offer funding and additional services that are geared toward training for employment and postsecondary education. Individuals with disabilities have unique VR needs based on their career employment outcomes and specific disabilities. Vocational rehabilitation services can include an array of services such as career counseling, academic education and training, and possibly medical and/or psychiatric treatment.

Policies for providing financial assistance to students with disabilities vary from state to state, depending in part on the resources available to the state VR agency: "To be eligible for services an individual must have an impairment that results in a substantial impediment to employment, and he/she must require VR services for employment" (HEATH Resource Center at the National Youth Transitions Center, 2015, p. 15). The local VR agency has counselors on staff who can work with a person with a disability to determine eligibility for services. They can also assist in coordinating and accessing needed services, which may be available through a postsecondary institution's disability services program or other agencies or community programs. Students should contact both the VR agency and the financial aid office of the institution they plan to attend as early as possible to be sure to meet all of the application deadlines.

Learning to Ask the Right Questions

1. Are private scholarships or grants available specifically for students with disabilities?
2. Is a vocational rehabilitation liaison available on the college campus?
3. Does the financial aid office offer assistance in completing financial aid forms?
4. When are the deadlines for applying for financial aid, and how early can the financial aid application process begin?

Learning to Ask the Right Questions, continued

5. Are the projected expenses at the college or university within the budget of your family?
6. What are the costs associated with attending the college or university in which you are interested (tuition, room and board, books, lab fees)?

Determining Class Sizes

Colleges have differing class sizes dependent upon the size of the college itself. Frequently, the class sizes are larger than what most students with disabilities experience during high school. Students often find themselves sitting in classrooms with more than 50 students. In some cases, classrooms may accommodate as many as 200–300 students. Larger class sizes may make it difficult for a student with a disability to establish a place within the classroom community. If you have been receiving a great deal of support or are used to individualized instruction, you may need to select a college that offers smaller class sizes. Some universities also require instructors teaching large classes to have multiple teaching assistants. Although this information may not be easy to find on the college's website, you usually can find out if large classes employ teaching assistants by asking this question during a campus visit. Teaching assistants not only aid professors in classroom management, but also often sponsor tutoring or small-group sessions to aid students in learning the class material.

Unlike teachers in the K–12 public school system, many professors do not have a mandatory attendance policy. If this is the case, students are solely responsible for managing their own attendance. Poor attendance often is less noted by professors who have a larger number of students. However, some universities do implement attendance policies for all classes. If you feel that mandatory attendance will help you to remain self-motivated, you will want to look for this type of policy when researching universities.

Student Disability Services Offices

Institutions of higher learning have Student Disability Services Offices (SDSOs), although they are referred to by other titles depending on the institution (e.g., Student Disability Service Center, Office of Student Accommodations, Office of Student Success and Disability Services, Student Disability Access Center, or Office of Educational Accessibility). SDSOs typically are located on the campus and provide a source of support for students with disabilities. When selecting a college, you should investigate the offerings that the disabilities office can provide. Some examples of services that may be available include:

- advocating for student rights,
- individual and group counseling designed for academic support for students with disabilities,
- study skills courses,
- tutors,
- counseling designed to address managing stress,
- assessment centers, and
- assistive technology resources, such as magnification systems like Zoom or 20/20 Spectrum for students with visual impairments, FM systems for students with hearing impairments, Open Book or JAWS programs (voice systems that orally read the text on a computer screen), text telephones, text-to-speech software, and audiobooks.

In addition to the services offered to students with disabilities, writing centers, advising centers, and reading centers may offer supports available to all students.

The key to maximize the supports offered through the SDSO is knowing what services are available and how to access these services. Students with disabilities are not automatically given accommodations, nor will a written invitation be extended to attend counseling sessions. You must be prepared to request accommodations and to determine which service offerings you will choose to participate in or utilize. When making the decision to attend a specific college, you should consider the offerings of the SDSO in relation to your specific disability and your needs. The following are some specific considerations that can be used to evaluate the SDSO and to determine how closely your needs are being met (Palmer, 2006):

> Where is the SDSO located?
> Are the office personnel familiar with your specific disability?
> Has the office served other students who have the same disability?
> If there is a support you need, is the office able to provide it?
> What documentation is required for accessing the services?
> Do staff members receive any special training?
> How many office staff are employed?
> How are services provided through the SDSO?
> What role does the SDSO play during freshman orientation?
> Does the SDSO offer training or education to faculty members regarding specific disability areas?
> Are faculty members required to participate in training regarding their responsibilities in working with students with disabilities?
> Who do parents contact if they have concerns during the school year?
> Does the SDSO provide support for students who need assistance in advocating for themselves (i.e., meeting with instructors)?

> ➤ Are there any support groups specifically designed to meet the needs of students who have been identified with your specific disability?

Samples of some of the forms that will be required for students with disabilities to receive services through the SDSO are included at the end of this chapter.

Learning to Ask the Right Questions

1. What are the levels of services offered through your university's Student Disability Services Office?
2. What is the process of obtaining accommodations through the SDSO? How are such accommodations determined?
3. What types of assistive technology devices are available to students with disabilities?
4. What additional resources are in place for students with disabilities?
5. Are staff members provided training, or do they have experience working with students with your specific disability?
6. If your specific disability directly impacts your ability to pass a required course, such as foreign language or mathematics, are course substitutions or waivers available?

Visiting College Campuses

After narrowing down college choices to two or three, it is highly recommended that you make appointments and visit the college campuses. During these visits, scheduled appointments with the Student Disability Services Office, financial aid office, and admissions office should be held. This provides you with the opportunity to ask specific questions and to determine how well your interests and skills match the colleges and/or universities that are being considered. The campus visit also provides opportunities for you to familiarize yourself with locations of the various support systems on campus.

Most colleges and universities provide tours of the campus where writing centers, reading centers, housing facilities, academic buildings, and social areas are identified. During the campus visit, students with disabilities should take the opportunity to talk with other students currently attending the college. Students enrolled in classes will be able to share information about classes, technology usage, professors, and extracurricular involvement. The college visit provides a firsthand opportunity to determine the "feel" of the campus. It is the most effective way to become familiar with the campus environment. What attitudes toward your disability are apparent? Does the campus feel too large or too small for you? How receptive do the professors seem toward students with disabilities?

Most colleges and universities provide an opportunity for a student to sit in on a class if requested. This opportunity allows a student with a disability to observe the format and level of difficulty of instruction, as well as the interactions between the students and the professor. Sitting in on instruction also will help you to determine if you are comfortable with the class size and the various environmental factors within the classroom setting.

Self-advocacy during the college admission process and later in life is a critical skill that students with disabilities must obtain. Prior to the campus visit you should focus on learning to ask the right questions. You should receive adequate instruction prior to interviewing at various colleges on how to actively advocate for yourself. When visiting colleges you need to be able to clearly articulate your disability and how your learning differences will affect the application process. You should be prepared to state your accommodation needs in functional, real-world terms, so that postsecondary institutions will be able to effectively accommodate your needs (HEATH Resource Center at the National Youth Transitions Center, 2006).

Understanding Admission Requirements: Preparing to Apply to College

Universities have specific admission criteria. When selecting a college or university, the first step is to ask whether or not the college has separate admission criteria for students with disabilities. Admission criteria for institutions vary and can include:

- submission of SAT or ACT scores that indicate a minimum standardized score,
- submission of letters of recommendation,
- minimum GPA in secondary school education, and
- submission of a short essay or reflection paper.

In addition, colleges may have a requirement for a minimum number of hours of foreign language to be completed in high school, but this is not the case in all colleges. Although there are minimum admission requirements for higher education, some colleges and universities may "consider the impact of the disability when making the admission decision" (Madaus, 2005, p. 34). However, this consideration is not required by law.

If SAT or ACT scores are required, you should review your PSAT scores (if you took it) and try to determine how you might perform on the SAT or ACT. Various computerized tutorial programs are available to assist you in preparing to take either exam. Note that the assessment situation itself can be quite intimidating with a testing allocation time of approximately 4 hours. Students with specific disabilities may need—or qualify for—special accommodations during the testing period. For the SAT, this option is available through the submission of a Student Eligibility Form to the Services for Students With Disabilities (SSD) Program of the College Board. Eligibility is based on documentation addressing seven guidelines (College Board, n.d.). Documentation must:

1. **State the specific disability, as diagnosed.** Diagnosis should be made by a person with appropriate professional credentials, should be specific, and when appropriate, should relate the disability to the applicable professional standards (e.g., the *DSM-5*; American Psychiatric Association, 2013).

2. **Be current.** In most cases, the evaluation and diagnostic testing should have taken place within 5 years of the request for accommodations.

3. **Provide relevant educational, developmental, and medical history.**

4. **Describe the comprehensive testing and techniques used to arrive at the diagnosis.** Include test results with subtest scores (standard or scaled scores) for all tests.

5. **Describe the functional limitations** (e.g., the limitations to learning impacted due to the diagnosed disability).

6. **Show that recommended accommodations are justified.** Describe the specific accommodations being requested on College Board tests.

7. **Establish the professional credentials of the evaluator** (e.g., licensure, certification, or area of specialization).

If you are eligible to obtain accommodations based on the approval of the College Board, accommodations in responding, presentation, setting, and timing may be requested. Additional information, including a more thorough list of accommodations and instructions on completing and submitting the required forms, can be obtained from the College Board at https://accommodations.collegeboard.org/documentation-guidelines/accommodations-documentation.

Some students with disabilities may struggle to meet the minimum test scores required or to produce an essay that fairly represents their ability to be successful in the college setting. Other students may struggle with achieving the required GPA while attending high school. Some institutions will recognize alternative testing formats or will accept supporting documentation to show academic achievement. It is recommended that students with disabilities include supplemental information indicating why specific requirements are not met. For example, if a student does not have minimum scores on the SAT, a statement should be included that specifically addresses how the disability directly impacts the score received. Providing information about a student's disability is a voluntary act. An institution of higher education cannot require that a student disclose their disability. Some states have made provisions to eliminate the need for students with disabilities to submit standardized testing scores for college admissions. For example, the Massachusetts Department of Higher Education (2019) stated that "Applicants with professionally diagnosed and documented learning disabilities (documentation must include diagnostic test results) are exempt from taking standardized tests for admission to any public institution of higher education in the Commonwealth" (p. 8). However, those universities and states with exemption policies may have alternative requirements that need to be met. We recommend that you check with your specific state and university while researching your college options.

Learning to Ask the Right Questions

1. What specific standardized assessments are required for college admittance?
2. Is there a minimum expectation for scores on standardized assessments (range of acceptable scores)?
3. Are special provisions made during the application process for students with disabilities?
4. Will additional supporting materials be accepted for special review if minimum university admittance criteria are not met?
5. Do you meet the expected academic criteria determined by the university (e.g., GPA)?

Online Education

More colleges and universities have entered into the online education space. Students can complete an associate, bachelor's, or master's degree online. In addition, many college campuses offer options to take a few courses within a degree plan online or take hybrid courses with a portion of the class offered online and a portion offered in the traditional face-to-face format. Students with identified disabilities should carefully consider whether to engage in online education. Although ADA does mandate that schools provide accommodations in the online learning environment, it does not specifically stipulate what that entails, and campuses tend to have varying approaches. When exploring online coursework options, students should consider multiple aspects of online education: the learning management system; course materials; assignments, group projects, and exams; professor and social interactions; and grading (EDsmart, 2016). Some students with specific disabilities find that online education proves to be a nonviable option for them, while others embrace the structure of such programs.

Parents may also want to consider factors when discussing online education programs with students. PACER's National Parent Center on Transition and Employment (2016) posted the following information:

> - Consider whether the online program has a point person for students with disabilities who is accessible to the student
> - Determine if there are readily available accommodations for students with disabilities
> - Investigate the accessibility of web-based tools used by the school and the cost, if any. Keep in mind that required software or computer operating system requirements are not considered accommodations in higher education
> - Understand that some online schools are "for profit" enterprises that have different entrance and payment criteria than traditional universities and colleges. Parents are urged to be

aware of programs that promise full degrees in short amounts of time

> Ask about the eligibility process for accessing accommodations, which may be more difficult to navigate when taking classes online
> Don't commit to paying tuition or sign a contract for an online class before you determine that necessary accommodations are available
> Find out if there is flexibility in the structure of an online program. For example, are there any alternative ways of presenting what you have learned, such as video presentations, live streaming, or others?
> Research how employers in your youth's field of study feel about online degrees; for example, some career fields, such as technology or social media, may embrace online learning, while more traditional fields, such as healthcare positions, may look more favorably on degrees granted in campus settings
> Verify the program completion and job-placement rates for graduates for the online program you are considering (p. 2)

There may also be some additional challenges for students with physical or sensory limitations in using digital material or completing assignments. These students must evaluate whether or not the learning management system is conducive to meeting their academic needs as students with a disability. In other words, does the system provide the accommodations needed for student success? If not, they may need to consider other schools. Additionally, there may be times when professors post content that is not accessible for students with a disability. Do not assume that your professor has an in-depth understanding of making content accessible. You are your greatest advocate, and you will need to be willing to discuss these issues with your professor so that you can reach a resolution.

Conclusion

Choosing a college that is right for you will affect your level of success and overall experience as a college student. You need to understand the expectations of the colleges you are interested in attending and how they match with your personal goals. Your needs and preferences in regard to academics, social opportunities, and financial considerations are important factors to consider. Taking the time to complete the Postsecondary Preference Worksheet at the end of this chapter also will help you narrow down your choices and direct you to the colleges that may be a better match for you. Just as important as the academic programs of a particular college is the logistical information about the college. Location, size of the college, and class size should be considered in making your decision, along with the services that are provided by the Student Disability Services Office. It is easy for students to want to go to a particular college because it is a popular college among their friends, but one college is not a fit for everyone. Figure 3 shares some common pitfalls students face when making decisions about which colleges to apply to and attend. Take the time to research and visit the colleges you choose so that you can make the decision that is right for you.

The end of this chapter includes some very important documents to review before attending college. The Disclosure Authorization Form, Student Intake Form, Test Form, and Disability Verification Form are sample documents to help you organize your information regarding your disability and education needs. It is a good idea to review these documents before you consider attending college so that you have a good idea of what gaps you will need to fill in your transition planning. These forms also can be used to compile information regarding your disability that can help you complete applications, scholarship forms, and other documents related to college.

Figure 3
Common Pitfalls for Students

"I'm applying to college X because all my friends are/are not going there."

"There's only one college that's right for me."

"All colleges are the same, so why bother with all this work?"

"I'm going to college X because my father/mother/sister/ brother went there (or wants me to go there)."

"College X is too expensive for me."

"I'm not applying there because I'll be rejected." (This does not mean you should avoid applying to one "long-shot" school.)

"If the one college I want doesn't want me, I'll be unhappy for the next 4 years."

Note. From *College Planning for Gifted Students: Choosing and Getting Into the Right College* (Updated ed., p. 94), by S. L. Berger, 2014, Taylor & Francis. Copyright 2014 by Taylor & Francis. Reprinted with permission.

Student Interviews

What process did you use in selecting the college you wanted to attend?

James: I didn't use a specific formal process, but I did begin by thinking about what career I would be interested in. Next, I researched all of the local universities within 3 hours of my parents' house that offered the degree I wanted. Because I didn't have much financial assistance, I wanted to choose a school with a high-quality education program but reasonable costs. I narrowed it down to three different schools, including Sam Houston State University (SHSU). The reason I chose SHSU was because they offered a great education program at an extremely reasonable cost. This decision-making process was relatively easy for me, because I had been well-prepared in high school for my self-advocacy role. I was also highly motivated to make my decision.

Jared: The process I used was simple. I knew that I didn't want to go to a large school and wanted to be on a smaller campus. I then determined the distance of how far the college was from my home. I didn't want to be too far away, but at the same time I did want to have some distance from home. My final decision was the University of Southern Mississippi.

Ricky: As a senior in high school, my process of selecting the college I wanted to attend was based on what I wanted to major in, which was turf management. I did not consider if a college had a program(s) in place to help a student with LD. My first and really only choice was University of Tennessee. When I didn't get accepted I was crushed. All of my friends were moving on to 4-year schools, and I had a feeling of being left behind. My parents suggested community college with the hope of getting some college credit under my belt and then transferring to a 4-year college. So that's what I did—attended one year of community college, and then I found out about Marshall University and their special program to support and tutor students with LD. After visiting there I felt that was going to be a perfect fit for me, and it was.

What role did examining career goals play in the selection of the university you attended?

James: The examination of career goals played a huge part in my selection of Sam Houston State University. This university is well known for being a high-quality education school, and several of my teachers and administrators in public school had attended SHSU and recommended it to me. Certain schools offer more extensive programs in certain areas, and part of preparing to self-advocate is to know how to identify the signs of a good program. One key point to keep in mind is that you want to avoid choosing a school based only on its good program. Other factors have to be considered, such as the size of the campus and its rigor. The university I selected was an appropriate match for me.

Jared: The University of Southern Mississippi has a very good computer engineering program, and that played a significant role in my decision to attend there.

Ricky: I based my decision to apply on what I thought I wanted to major in. At the time I wanted to study turf management, and I knew that University of Tennessee had one of the few programs in the country. After failing to get in there and following a year of community college, I attended Marshall University and decided that what I really wanted to do was become a teacher and a coach, so I majored in education and teaching students with LD like myself.

What specific college options did you research?

James: Postsecondary education offers many different options for a student depending on what your needs are. Some students need a great deal of support and must attend school close to home. As much as I wanted to leave home and spread my wings, I knew that I needed to be somewhat close to my parents' house for both emotional and financial support. In many ways the idea of a community or junior college appealed to me, but on the same token I couldn't become a fully certified teacher through those institutions. I enrolled in SHSU, but I was still not sure if it was the right choice until I met the faculty in my department. One professor in particular, Dr. Simpson, was very welcoming, and I couldn't wait to take classes in the special education program. This confirmed my choice and helped ease my tension about coming to a 4-year school.

Ricky: My goal was always to go to a 4-year university, and I knew I wanted to go away to school, live in a dorm, and live the college experience. Our local community college had an option with the state schools that after completing 2 years you could transfer to a state school without having to take the SAT again. I thought that may be a path for me, but then I discovered Marshall University and transferred after only one year of community college.

What types of questions did the Student Disability Services Office answer for you?

James: They were very helpful. I scheduled my appointment with them and asked my social coach to accompany me. They answered several minor questions, but the most important questions were related to what services the office could provide. I knew what I needed in high school, but I was not sure in regard to college, because I had never experienced it before. My social coach and parents helped me come up with some ideas and questions to ask, and these served as a guide in the meeting. What I've learned is that the best approach to take is to develop a list of 5–10 questions prior to the interview. This serves as a way to help you remember what is important and to get the most out of the meeting. In a way, this meeting serves as an interview between the institution and you to establish what they are able to do for you. In essence, you are hiring the school to support you on their campus.

Angela: The main thing I needed to know was what to do each semester to get my accommodations. I feel that the Student Disability Services Office pretty much answered any question I had for them.

Ricky: After meeting with the people at the H.E.L.P. Center, they assured me and my parents that this program really covered all of the bases for me. I would have to be retested because my IEP had expired, but that was easily done. Their program included tutors for all or any classes I needed and extended times for tests. They helped me organize my time and stay on track with daily updates and progress, and reported all of this back to my parents. If I missed any tutoring time it was reported, but that was not really an issue for me because I was totally committed to this program and how they could help me complete my 4 years.

How many colleges did you visit, and what did you gain from the college campus visit?

James: After reviewing around 10 colleges and universities, I chose three colleges to visit. I gained a general understanding of the college life and culture on each campus, which helped me to make informed decisions about what I liked and didn't like. Afterward, I made a pros and cons list for each campus and compared them to each other based on 10 criteria that were important to me.

Jared: I visited around five colleges, and each one felt different from the last one. Just by walking around I was able to tell how the college community worked and which ones felt welcoming.

When did you determine that you had to become an advocate for yourself?

James: I made that choice during my junior year of high school when my IEP team began to discuss transition. They explained to me that I had to start making some of my own academic decisions at age 18, because I would be in charge of my IEP meetings. Again, this was a choice I had to make. My parents could no longer decide for me, even though they continued to encourage me.

Angela: There was a particular incident that occurred that made me realize that I had to become an advocate for myself. I think this realization came the day I moved into my dorm room. I realized I was on my own when my family left after moving me in my room. This was also when I had some anxieties about beginning college. I was worried about quite a few things, such as being away from home, which was very hard for me at first, as well as the workload and the level of difficulty of work. I was also worried about tests because I have bad test anxiety.

Ricky: I sort of self-advocated for myself starting in the third grade. I had a wonderful teacher who recognized my struggles and suggested the 504 plan for me. She also let me go to the reading specialist in the school with the other kids already in the program. I was never shy or felt embarrassed about asking for help and verbalizing what I needed. I was also very respectful to my teachers and tried to find common ground with them.

How did learning to ask the right questions help you in the college planning process?

James: I didn't always know the right questions to ask. In the beginning, I relied mostly on professionals and my parents for guidance. Unfortunately, public school doesn't prepare students very well for self-advocacy. Teachers and counselors discussed transition and what they planned to do to help me, but they didn't actually provide tangible resources or help in regard to my learning to ask questions.

Jared: I learned in high school that there is no such thing as a bad question. You need to speak what is on your mind, and if you have a question, ask it. If you don't speak up, you might find yourself unhappy with your decision.

Ricky: When I met with the people at the H.E.L.P. Center I was mostly concerned with what resources were available to me. I knew what resources I had in high school, but I didn't know what I'd be entitled to in college.

After you determined what university you would attend, what types of anxieties did you experience, if any?

James: The most severe anxiety I felt was related to the prospect of going to a new school and being away from my parents. For the most part I was ready to go, but I think my parents were worried as well. We didn't know what to expect; we had never done this [attending college with a disability] before. The huge benefit I had was that my brother was already attending SHSU, and he had allowed me to spend the night on campus to get used to the idea. My preparation, along with my brother's support, allowed me to do well and experience a marginal level of anxiety. Preparation is the key!

Jared: When I chose what university I would be going to I didn't really feel any anxiety. I felt relieved that I made the decision. I was very excited to be going to college.

Ricky: Even though I was excited to be going away to school, I was also anxious about being on my own. I worried about being able to keep up with the level of academics and being a successful student. I didn't know anyone there, but once I started class and started making friends and got a feel for the level of support, my anxieties lessened.

Once you made the decision to attend the university you selected, did you celebrate? How did you feel?

James: Absolutely, I was ecstatic. I realized that all of the years of struggling, hard work, and personal dedication were finally paying off and my dreams of being a teacher might actually happen. Despite all of the people that were cheering me on, I didn't believe I could do it until the end of my first semester at SHSU when I received my grades. I got a 4.0. I couldn't believe it. In many ways, I had begun to realize what a famous professor once said: "We cannot change the cards we are dealt, just how we play the hand." I was dealt Asperger's syndrome, and what I played was victory over it.

Jared: I was so happy that I made the decision to attend University of Southern Mississippi. I felt that I had a weight lifted off my chest once I made the decision.

Ricky: I just felt happiness that I finally had achieved a goal that I had set. I had experienced a few setbacks and twists and turns along the way, but the road had finally led to getting my college degree. It was well worth it.

Postsecondary Preference Worksheet

Name of college or university: _____

Academic Characteristics	Student Comments
Highly competitive academically	
Moderately competitive	
Not competitive	
Average SAT/ACT score	
High school GPA of current freshman class	
Other	

Demographics	Student Comments
Size of city/town	
Size of college	
Distance from home	
Public transportation	
Parking facilities	
Access to buildings	
Food services	
Other	

Admission Policies	Student Comments
Minimum ACT or SAT scores	
Admission requirements	
College essay	
Specific course requirements	
Teacher recommendation letters	
Other	

Postsecondary Preference Worksheet, continued

Field of Study	Student Comments
Availability of major	
Admission requirements for major	
Full-time years of study for completion	
Part-time years of study for completion	

Services for Students With Disabilities	Student Comments
Student Disability Services Office	
Study-skills classes	
Time-management classes	
Developmental academic classes	
Career placement services	
Note-takers	
Assistive technology	
Computer availability	
Alternative formats for course materials	
Extended time for tests	
Alternate tests administration	
Other	

Housing	Student Comments
Residence halls	
Off-campus housing	
Substance-free residence halls	

Postsecondary Preference Worksheet, continued

Housing, continued	Student Comments, continued
Single-gender halls	
Coed halls	
Quiet designated study hours	
Internet access in rooms/ residence halls	
Cooking facilities available	
Visitation hours	
Other	
Campus Life	Student Comments
Clubs or organizations of interest	
Sports activities	
Health clinic	
Fitness center	
Counseling center	
Computer labs	
Other	

Disclosure Authorization Form

Student: _____

Student ID#:_____

I authorize the Student Disability Services Office/Disability Resource Center at any university to:

❏ Exchange with   ❏ Disclose to   ❏ Obtain from

Name and/or Organization Address: _____

The following information:

❏ Psychological Evaluations   ❏ Neuropsychological Evaluations
❏ Psychological/Psychiatric Evaluations ❏ Medical Records
❏ *Other*

For the following purpose(s): _____

_____

_____

_____   _____
Signature of Student   *Date*

_____   _____
Witness   *Date*

I understand that my records are protected under federal and state confidentiality laws and regulations.

Student Intake Form

Student's Name: _____

Date: _____ ID#: _____

Contact Information

Mailing Address:

Street: _____

City: _____ State: _____ Zip: _____

Permanent Address:

Street: _____

City: _____ State: _____ Zip: _____

Phone: _____ Cell: _____

Email: _____

Area of Study:

Major: _____

Check One:

❏ Freshman   ❏ Sophomore   ❏ Junior   ❏ Senior
❏ Law Student   ❏ Graduate

1. What is your diagnosed disability?

   _____

   _____

   _____

2. Describe your disability and how it affects your performance as a student.

   _____

   _____

   _____

Student Intake Form, continued

3. List the accommodations you are requesting.

   _____

   _____

   _____

4. List any accommodations that you have received in the past.

   _____

   _____

   _____

5. List any assistive technology that you have used in the past.

   _____

   _____

   _____

6. Is there any additional information that you would like for us to know regarding your accommodations?

   _____

   _____

   _____

Test Form

Location: Student Building
DSO Testing Hours: Monday–Friday: 8:00 a.m.–8:00 p.m.
Phone: (_____)____-_____ **Fax:** (_____)____-_____

Completed form MUST BE RETURNED TO THE DSO AT LEAST ONE WEEK prior to the date of the exam. In order to receive testing accommodation, you must have all sections completed. You may only receive the accommodations allowed and the materials allowed by your professor.

SECTION A: To be completed by the student.
All exams are to be taken during the DSO Testing Hours stated above.

Test Date: _____ Test Time: _____

Name: _____

Email: _____ Phone: _____

Course & Section #: _____

Instructor: _____

Accommodations Needed:

❑ Extended Time: _____ ❑ Taped Format

❑ Quiet/Distraction Free Room   ❑ Scribe   ❑ Word Processor

❑ Reader

❑ Other: _____

_____   _____
Signature of Student   Date

Disability Verification Form

THIS FORM IS TO BE COMPLETED BY A LICENSED PROFESSIONAL

This student may be eligible for special accommodations at this college. In order to provide services, we must have documentation of a disability that impairs one or more major life functions. Please complete the form and submit to:

_____

Student Name: _____

SS#: _____

Please provide the following information in full (please be specific). This form is not valid without a specific diagnosis and description of the disability, the functional limitations as a result of the disability, and the signature, date, and license number of the professional evaluator.

Disability/Diagnosis: _____

Description of assessments and methods used to make the diagnosis:

_____

_____

_____

Description of the disability:

_____

_____

_____

Disability Verification Form, continued

In what settings or on what academic tasks will this disability likely manifest itself?

_____

_____

_____

Recommendations for services and accommodations:

❏ extended time on tests   ❏ preferential seating
❏ note-taker   ❏ taped textbooks
❏ computer   ❏ tape recorder
❏ alternate testing environment   ❏ alternate testing format
❏ scribe   ❏ reader
❏ calculator   ❏ other

Prescribed medications, dosage, side effects:

_____

_____

I certify that all the information on this form is true and correct to the best of my knowledge.

_____   _____
Signature of Licensed Professional   _Date_

_____
Print Name

_____
Title or License Type and Number

_____
Contact Information

4

Preparing to Attend College

The Application Process

Once you have narrowed down the list of colleges that you are interested in applying to, you will need to begin the application process. It is typically recommended that you apply to at least six colleges—two "reach" colleges that are more selective academically, two colleges where acceptance is likely, and two colleges where admittance is guaranteed. Most colleges will refer you to the college's website to download the application forms or to complete them through an online portal. These forms take time to complete and will include some deadlines for submission. This chapter includes a College Application Timeline checklist that you can use to assist you in a timely completion of your application. Counselors and college coaches are good resources to help with the application process.

 DOI: 10.4324/9781003233749-5

Writing the College Essay

Some colleges may require that you include a college essay or writing sample. This may seem overwhelming if you have difficulty with writing, but there is plenty of assistance to help you with this part of the application. Do not shy away from applying to certain colleges just because you have to write an essay to be accepted. Remember that this is only one part of the application. The following are some helpful tips in writing a college essay.

> - Review a couple of books on college essays. This will give you some insight into what the colleges may be looking for.
> - Discuss some possible topics with your English teacher. Some senior English classes work on students' college essays during the first part of the year. If not, consider using a tutor to help with the writing process or ask a teacher for help before or after school.
> - Be original! Give the admissions officers something fun to read.
> - Have someone look over your paper. Get feedback on what needs to be improved.
> - Revise and rewrite.

Figure 4 provides insight into what colleges look for in a good essay.

Requesting Letters of Recommendation

Another necessary part of the application will be the letters of recommendation. You will need to ask at least two high school staff members (e.g., the school counselor and a teacher) and possibly an employer or close friend of the family to write a letter of recommendation. Some students also ask community leaders, such as the head

Figure 4
What Colleges Look for in Admissions Essays

› Writing ability	› Capacity for growth
› Intellectual curiosity	› Leadership potential
› Initiative and motivation	› Community service
› Creativity	› Consistency with other elements of the student's application
› Self-discipline	
› Character	

Note. From *College Planning for Gifted Students: Choosing and Getting Into the Right College* (Updated ed., p. 170), by S. L. Berger, 2014, Taylor & Francis. Copyright 2014 by Taylor & Francis. Reprinted with permission.

of a nonprofit they've been involved with or a religious group leader, to write letters of recommendation. Always remember that those you request a letter from should know you well—especially those who are not your teachers.

Sometimes the application will include a form that needs to be completed by the person writing the recommendation, so you will want to make sure you have read the directions thoroughly before you complete this step. In order to assist those who will be writing the letter of recommendation, you also should type up a one-page handout that shows your GPA, organizations and club memberships, and school and community activities, as well as any other information that you would like mentioned in the letter. This ensures that the information in the letter will be a true reflection of your accomplishments. It also helps you develop a resume for potential employment.

Making the Right Choice

Once the acceptance letters begin to arrive, you will need to begin deciding on which school is the right match for you. Unfortunately, you will probably receive a few letters that tell you that you have been wait-listed or even denied admittance, but keep in mind that most students rarely get an acceptance letter for every application they submit. It is normal to be disappointed, but do not take it personally. The college may have had an unusually large amount of applicants or only a specific number of spaces available. Even so, you should feel proud that you put forth the effort to apply to a variety of colleges. By doing so, you gave yourself some choice in selecting the college that is the right fit for you.

On a rare occasion, a student may not be accepted to any of the colleges to which they apply. If this happens to you, the next step would be to apply to a community college for the first 2 years of study and then transfer to a 4-year college once you have proven yourself as a capable student. The transfer process often is more cost effective and still allows you to achieve the same end goals.

Learning to Ask the Right Questions

1. Have you chosen the colleges that you want to apply to?
2. Have you accessed or requested an application from each of those colleges?
3. Have you reviewed the College Application Timeline checklist so you can meet all of the deadlines?
4. Have you written your college essay?
5. Have you asked teachers, employers, and colleagues to write a letter of recommendation?
6. Have you prepared your one-page handout to assist the persons writing the letters of recommendation?
7. Have you chosen the college that you will attend?

Disability Services Coordinator

One of the main differences between college and high school is that in the college setting the student is responsible for initiating or beginning the process of requesting accommodations for coursework. After being accepted into the college of your choice, you should determine if you will disclose information regarding your disability to the university. Some students with disabilities feel that they can successfully experience college life without the use of additional supports and services. However, most students with disabilities find it beneficial to disclose their disability to the Disability Services Coordinator and begin to lay the foundation for receiving support services. Professors on college campuses see many students enter into programs without disclosing their disability. Some of these students struggle with the day-to-day responsibilities of time management. The decision to self-disclose is a personal one. Great consideration to this decision should be given, and ultimately the decision should be left to you.

A critical question that you should ask yourself when determining whether or not to disclose your disability is, "Will I benefit from attending a university or college without academic accommodations?" If you find that you will not receive a direct benefit from attending without accommodations, then you should consider the following questions as well:

> How significant is the disability?
> How much does the nature or manifestation of the disability conflict with the needs of the educational program?
> How open is the educational program to recognizing and accommodating individuals with disabilities?

It is imperative to understand that if you choose not to disclose your disability, then the institution will not be accountable for providing academic accommodations or supports. If you determine that you will disclose your disability, then the next step would be to begin that process. To initiate this process, you should set up an appointment to visit with the Disability Services Coordinator, who can assist you in understanding the process to receive accommodations and other services specifically related to your disability. If you do not contact the Disability Services Coordinator and provide the required documentation, you will not receive accommodations. In addition, you should be sure to ask how often an application for accommodations needs to be filed. Is it per semester, term, or academic year?

The Disability Services Coordinator will need you to be prepared to present the required documentation forms. Most colleges and universities request information such as your high school IEP and most recent comprehensive evaluation. This may include the diagnostic report for your disability, which can be obtained from your school psychologist, educational diagnostician, or medical doctor. If your most recent assessment is more than 3 years old, the college or university may request that additional testing be done to determine whether or not you will be eligible for accommodations in the college setting. Some universities offer counseling centers where the assessment can be done for an additional fee. After reviewing the required documentation forms, the Disability Services Coordinator will work with you to determine which accommodations are needed. Remember that the law does not require that all accommodations given in high school also be offered in the college or university setting. You should be prepared to explain how your specific disability impacts your learning and which accommodations will assist you in becoming more academically successful. Chapter 5 focuses on accommodations and academic success.

The Virginia Department of Education (2003) recommended that students practice responding to the following questions prior to their meeting with the Disability Services Coordinator:

> Can you describe your educational background?
> Can you describe your disability?
> What are your strengths and weaknesses, in and outside the classroom?
> What adaptive equipment are you currently using?
> What training did you receive in using this adaptive equipment?
> Who provided your technical support?
> How did you communicate with your instructors about using your adaptive equipment in the classroom? How did they respond?

> What appropriate academic adjustments and auxiliary aids and services do you have to assist you for class?
> Explain how your accommodations have made you successful. (p. 32)

Your response to these questions will assist the Disability Services Coordinator in making recommendations for services and accommodations that are best matched to your individual needs.

Learning to Ask the Right Questions

1. Where is the Student Disability Services Office located?
2. Who is the Disability Services Coordinator you will be meeting with?
3. How soon can an appointment be scheduled to meet with the Disability Services Coordinator?
4. Do you have all of the necessary forms that will be needed to document your disability? Are they all located in one easy-to-find place?
5. Are you prepared to answer the necessary questions in an effort to advocate for yourself?

Release of Information

At the time of the meeting with the Disability Service Coordinator, students with disabilities will find that the role of the parent differs from the role played during high school. Parents are limited in their ability to communicate with the college or university without the written consent of the student. For some students it may be necessary to give written consent for parents to be able to communicate with the college or university. Depending on the specific disability that you have, you may find it difficult to communicate effectively about financial matters, accommodations, safety concerns, and other college-related issues. Thus, this may be information that your parents could effectively communicate or advocate for on your behalf.

Many students with disabilities sign a release of information so that the university or college can legally communicate with parents regarding progress (including student grades). Throughout the high school years, many parents are very active in the planning of their child's IEP. In postsecondary education, as the student, you are responsible for making sure that you are following the correct degree plans and making necessary payments to the college and university. Handling such matters may be overwhelming without strong self-advocacy skills.

Learning to Ask the Right Questions

1. Is a standard form available to request a release of information?
2. What information can be shared with the identified person listed on the release form?
3. Are you prepared to advocate for yourself in regard to financial and academic matters if a release of information form is not signed?
4. Do you have the time management and organization skills needed to maintain designated timelines for tuition payments and eligibility timelines?

Freshman Orientation Programs

Prior to the start of the semester, students will be provided with information on their university's freshman orientation. Some colleges have orientation earlier in the summer, but for many colleges it takes place a few days prior to the beginning of the fall semester. This gives you and your parents a little extra time to familiarize yourselves with your new living and academic environment. At many universities, students also will be given a resource packet that will include information regarding all aspects of university life and academic life (more generic information on university life can be found in Chapter 6).

For a student with a disability, freshman orientation provides the opportunity to reduce anxiety, obtain valuable information about student services, become oriented with the university campus, and begin to develop friendships with other new students. The Student Disability Services Office may offer an additional orientation for students with disabilities in which more in-depth service support information is shared. Regardless of the orientation that students attend, the experience is extremely meaningful for students with disabilities. We highly recommend attending a freshman orientation session.

Often freshman orientation (sometimes called a freshman weekend or camp) involves an overnight stay on the campus before the school year starts. Freshman weekends typically involve students staying at one of the campus dormitories. For students with a specific disability, this overnight stay provides a glimpse of what dorm life and/or independent living is like. Resident Assistants (RAs) are typically involved in the dormitory experience. Making contact with the designated RA that will be living in your dorm will allow you to communicate your needs prior to the first official moving day.

Another positive aspect of the freshman orientation experience is utilizing time after the campus tour to locate where specific classes are held. Orientation staff members typically are available to assist students in finding classrooms and performing "trial runs" of their schedule. Most students, regardless of whether or not they have a disability, express concerns about getting lost on campus or arriving late to class. This dry run will allow you to be more comfortable with traveling across campus.

In addition to having the opportunity to discuss living arrangements with the RA, students often are provided with preplanned social activities. The social activities are designed to facilitate opportunities for students to meet each other and develop friendships, as well as experience university life and create school spirit. These activities are great ways to meet other incoming students without the pressure of the first days of school. At several campuses, students involved with student government or student activities attend the events and offer insight on the day-to-day college experience. We encourage students to take advantage of all of the activities they feel comfortable attending—this experience can go a long way toward preparing you to start your university career.

Learning to Ask the Right Questions

1. Have you read all of the information regarding your university's freshman orientation?
2. Do you know what paperwork and personal belongings you will need to bring to orientation?
3. If an overnight stay is required for freshman orientation, are private rooms available or needed?
4. Is a separate parents' orientation offered?
5. Will the Student Disability Services Office offer a special orientation for students with disabilities?

Housing Accommodations

Deciding where to live can be both exciting and challenging, and there are many considerations in making the best possible choice for you. College success depends on attending classes and fulfilling the requirements of each course. If you have a physical disability that requires additional time to get from place to place, it may be more practical for you to live on campus close to the academic buildings, dining hall, library, computer lab, and other necessary facilities. If you have decided to live at home, you will want to research transportation options. You may want to consider where parking is located or if shuttle services are available from the dormitory or apartment to the location where your program of study is offered. If you will be walking to class, you will want to check on the distance you will need to walk and determine if you are physically able to handle the length of the walk.

When considering housing arrangements, keep in mind that the place you lives extends beyond the place you sleep. Electing to live in the dormitory poses benefits as well as risks for a student with a disability. Frequently, dormitory settings have unspoken rules regarding social interaction among students living in the same building and sharing facilities. For some disability areas, this can be a challenge.

Other challenges that may be encountered include the lack of structured quiet times or study hours. Some colleges and university housing facilities offer study rooms or study halls in which a quieter environment can be expected. In addition to studying, students may need to overcome the desire for privacy when taking care of hygiene. Dorm settings may be designed with communal restroom facilities, meaning that all students on a floor or in a block of rooms are expected to shower in restrooms allocated on each floor. However, some dorms offer suites or private restroom facilities.

In addition, many housing contracts include dining options. If you are a student with specific nutritional needs, you can go to the college or university website to explore what type of dining options are available. Many campus dining facilities now offer more healthy eating options for students who may have specific food allergies or who may be vegan or vegetarian. They may also provide nutritional information to assist students in making healthy food choices.

If you are living on campus, you may find that additional housing accommodations may be required. If additional accommodations are needed, you should contact the Disability Services Coordinator to make the request for the accommodations. Additional accommodations that the university or college may be able to provide include wheelchair-accessible bathtubs and rooms (for students with orthopedic impairments), Braille numbering (for students with visual impairments), and/or strobe lighting (for students with hearing impairments).

Another issue that tends to be overlooked is the need for laundry facilities. Students often have their laundering needs met at home during the elementary and high school years. If this has been the case, learning to operate coin-operated laundry machines should be taken care of prior to attendance at college. Most apartments either have washers and dryers in the apartment or, like dorms, have designated laundry facilities for the entire community to share.

The Housing Checklist at the end of this chapter can be used to collect and keep records of the housing accommodations for each institution. There is also enough space in the "Yes" column for additional notes. Using this type of checklist will help narrow your choices and assist you in the decision-making process regarding college housing options.

Learning to Ask the Right Questions

1. How far from campus are the living facilities located, and are you able to manage the distance needed to walk to campus?
2. If shuttles are used at the campus, where are shuttle pick-up stops located, and where can you find the shuttle schedule? Are there fees associated with this service?
3. If you choose to live off campus and have to drive to campus, is parking available near the buildings in which you will be attending class?
4. Do the facilities in which you choose to live have a location in which "study rules" apply (e.g., a separate room or designated floor)?
5. If living in a dorm, are female and male students housed separately? Are there restrictions on visitation hours and curfews?
6. Does a resident advisor live in the building, and, if so, how are they accessed? What is their designated role within the building?

Choosing a Roommate

Choosing a roommate can be a difficult process: "It has been shown that a student's relationship with his/her roommate has a significant impact on the student's college experience, particularly for first year students" (Knapp et al., 2004, p. 211). Most college housing departments give incoming freshmen a questionnaire to match them with compatible roommates. Some of these questionnaires will ask general questions about your living and study habits, although others are very detailed and specific. Either way, it is important to answer all questions honestly. In other words, you need to complete the form. Schools typically will try to match up lifestyles, so the more information they have, the better the chances that you will be placed with someone who is compatible with you. Issues dealing with neatness, sleeping habits, and noise level may seem minor, but they can make a big difference in a successful college experience. An example of a roommate questionnaire can be found at the end of this chapter. You also may choose to select your roommate from a friend, classmate, or family member already attending or also entering the college. This can provide a level of comfort that an unknown roommate does not. However, many of the same ideas about compatibility still apply.

A student with a disability such as ASD may struggle with social interactions when sharing a dormitory room with another individual. Some students prefer to have a single occupancy room. When you apply for housing, the housing department needs to be informed of this request if this is your preference. Students with disabilities should be prepared to provide documentation that supports the need for a single occupancy room (social and sensory issues should be addressed in the documentation). If single occupancy rooms are available, they may have an additional fee attached to them.

Other students with disabilities find that dormitory living, even if a single occupancy room is available, does not meet their individual needs. Living off campus in an apartment is also an option that can be examined. This provides you with the opportunity to socialize according to your own timeframe. You also will have the opportunity to avoid social expectations often encountered in a dormitory setting. However, you will be expected to take care of responsibilities such as paying rent and bills on time that are covered in your single fee for dormitory living. With many of the other choices you will have to make about your college experience, the various housing options must be weighed carefully.

Regardless of your best efforts to select a compatible roommate, issues with your roommate might occur. Some of the following are tips that students have provided that have helped them in both preventing and problem solving conflicts with roommates:

➤ Sign a roommate contract.
➤ Be willing to comprise when disagreements occur.
➤ Respect each other's boundaries.
➤ Accept your own faults and take responsibility for them.
➤ Honestly communicate with each other.
➤ Socialize with other friends.
➤ Keep your space clean.
➤ Take care of your personal hygiene.
➤ Respect the views and opinions of your roommate even though they may be different than your own.
➤ Don't "borrow" your roommate's food, clothing, or personal items without asking first.
➤ Work out a schedule for sleeping and studying. This is especially important if you're a morning person and your roommate is a night person.
➤ Be courteous and polite to your roommate—say "thank you" and don't be afraid to say, "I am sorry."

Learning to Ask the Right Questions

1. Is the roommate I am selecting socially compatible with me (cleanliness, study habits, waking and bed times, etc.)?

Learning to Ask the Right Questions, continued

2. Are single occupancy rooms available if a roommate situation is not appropriate? If so, what are the fees associated
with this, and what is the process for requesting single
occupancy rooms?

Conclusion

Narrowing down your options is only the first step in getting
into the college of your choice. The next step is the application process, and it is going to take a lot of work and commitment on your
part to make sure the application is complete and submitted on time.
Using the College Application Timeline as a checklist to keep you on
track will ensure that you meet all required deadlines. Once you have
been accepted and have chosen the college you will attend, you will
have to decide on whether or not to disclose your disability. Most
students find it beneficial to disclose their disability so that they can
receive the academic supports they will need to perform up to their
academic potential. The sooner you contact the Student Disability
Services Office, the more prepared the staff will be to make sure you
receive the requested accommodations.

Another critical decision that has to be made at this point
involves your housing arrangements. It is important to be honest
when completing the questionnaire to be matched with a roommate,
but it is your decision if, when, and how to disclose your disability to
your roommate. Just remember, honesty is probably the best policy
in being able to live together and accommodate each other's differences in regard to personality, learning styles, and habits.

Student Interviews

How did you decide on your living arrangements for college?

James: With much difficulty, we debated the pros and cons of having and not having a roommate. Fortunately, I had an option that represented an in-between for me. My brother Greg was living in a house that had extra unused bedrooms, and by rooming with him, I was getting a roommate, but it was one I knew very well. Now that I look back at that decision, I feel we made the right choice. When I was first starting college, the last thing we wanted was for an issue like a roommate to become a problem, and because of our choice, it didn't. It allowed me to focus on classes and my living skills without the pressure of a new person.

Angela: I lived in a dorm the first year and then an apartment the rest of the time. The first 2 years I did not choose my roommates, and then after that I started rooming with people I had met while in classes. My dorm roommate was the best roommate placement ever, and we have become great friends. Even though I'm pretty easygoing and easy to get along with, the roommates I thought would be great ended up not working out. However, I do think it is a great idea to room with someone of similar interests and majors.

Ricky: I didn't really have to decide on my living arrangements. The first year they were made for me. After that I got an apartment and roomed with the friends I had made.

What factors did you consider in choosing a roommate?

James: Because I really didn't have one, except for my brother, this is a tough question. However, I did think about this in case the situation didn't work out. My biggest concerns were shared bathrooms, social life, and cleanliness. I didn't want a really messy roommate or one that held a party at our place every other night. In addition, the idea of sharing a bathroom was scary because I have very particular grooming rituals and a resistance to changes in my schedule. This is an area to which all college students should give careful consideration.

Jared: I really didn't care what kind of roommate I got. I just wanted to be sure that he would be neat. I didn't want a really messy roommate.

Ricky: One of my roommates was in the H.E.L.P. program, too, but I also made friends just from being in class with them.

Did you disclose your disability to your roommate?

Angela: Once I got to know my roommate I informed her of my disability just by explaining what it was and what I have problems with, along with examples of what it is like to deal with these issues.

Jared: I ended up not having a roommate, but when I got to know friends really well, I told them about my disability.

What suggestions would you have for students who are trying to decide on living arrangements, including decisions on roommates?

James: I would suggest four things . . .
1. Be open to the idea of a roommate, given you can reach some compromises.
2. Don't be afraid to communicate your needs and concerns because you have to live there for a year, and you don't want to feel uncomfortable in your own home.
3. Try to resolve any disagreements with your roommate first before going to your parents or your school because if you leave them out, they will feel like you didn't give them a chance.

4. Look at all living options, both on campus and off, because often off-campus living is more adjustable and leasing office personnel tend to work with you more because you are seen as a customer. Also, off-campus living is not always more expensive, but on the same token it is not always as nice.

Ricky: I think that depends on your disability and personality. For example, if you need quiet time or study late, you may try to find a student with similar requirements. I think if you are open about your disability and can communicate and compromise, it could be a situation that has a very positive experience.

Do you have any helpful tips for living with a roommate?

James: I would encourage being honest and open with your roommate about your needs and your disability. [They] may be much more willing to accommodate you if you are honest and relaxed. Despite the issues that occur with roommates, some of the best college friendships happen because of your living arrangements, so don't feel like you have to be a stranger; you may have a lot in common. Remember that half of your college education is not in your classrooms, but in your social life and the friendships that you make.

Angela: I think that even if you do choose your roommates, they don't always turn out like you think they would. Regardless of whom you live with, you have to make the best of it and understand that everyone is different.

Ricky: Communicate and compromise. Not everyone will see situations as you do, not everyone has the same interpretation or experiences, but that is part of learning to live in a world of diversity. I think most people can accept honesty and compromise.

College Application Timeline

Directions: Use this timeline to help keep track of the application process. Check off each item once it is completed.

September
- ❏ Choose the colleges that you would like to attend.
- ❏ Review college applications.
- ❏ Request a copy of your high school transcript.
- ❏ Type up a one-page handout that shows your GPA, organizations and club memberships, school and community activities, and any other information that may be helpful for those persons writing the letters of recommendation.

October
- ❏ Begin filling out the college applications.
- ❏ Mark the deadline for each college application on your calendar.
- ❏ Ask for letters of recommendation from two high school staff members and possibly an employer or family friend.
- ❏ Take the SAT or ACT again if you want to improve your previous scores.
- ❏ Complete the college essay or writing sample.
- ❏ Research possible scholarships and financial aid.

November–December
- ❏ Submit college applications before the deadline.
- ❏ Continue to research possible scholarships.

January
- ❏ Complete and submit the Free Application for Federal Student Aid (FAFSA) starting January 1 if you are interested in receiving financial assistance.

February–March
- ❏ If you have not received notification of receipt, contact the colleges to confirm that they received your application.

College Application Timeline, continued

April–May

❏ Based on your acceptance and rejection or wait-list letters, make your decision about which college you want to attend.

❏ Submit required paperwork and deposits to confirm that you are accepting the school's offer. You may include your documentation required by the Student Disability Services Office if you are seeking accommodations, or you may schedule an appointment to meet with them.

❏ Visit the college you will be attending.

Housing Checklist

University: _____

Are the following options available? If so, is there anything you should remember about the options that could help in the decision-making process?

Residence halls	❏ No	❏ Yes
Ease of accessibility	❏ No	❏ Yes
Tobacco- and alcohol-free residence halls	❏ No	❏ Yes
Single occupancy rooms	❏ No	❏ Yes
Coed halls	❏ No	❏ Yes
Male-only/female-only halls	❏ No	❏ Yes
Visitation hours	❏ No	❏ Yes
Study areas in residence halls	❏ No	❏ Yes
Quiet hours in residence halls	❏ No	❏ Yes
Computers in residence halls	❏ No	❏ Yes
Cooking facilities available	❏ No	❏ Yes
Dining facilities/accessibility	❏ No	❏ Yes
Off-campus housing/costs	❏ No	❏ Yes
Accessibility of commute to campus	❏ No	❏ Yes
Parking for student	❏ No	❏ Yes
Public transportation	❏ No	❏ Yes

Sample Roommate Questionnaire

This form is designed to help our office match you with a roommate. Please answer the questions as accurately as possible. If there is someone in particular with whom you would like to room, please include their name on this form. Roommate assignments will be made on July 1. We will do our best to fill your request.

PLEASE TYPE OR PRINT

Name: _____ Gender:_____

Street: _____

City: _____ State: _____ Zip: _____

Phone: _____ Cell:_____

Current Email Address: _____

Do you already have someone you would like to room with? ❏ Yes ❏ No

If yes, please give their name and contact information:

_____

Tell Us About You

Music:

What type of music do you listen to? _____

_____

Do you listen to music when studying/in your room? *(check all that apply)*
❏ yes   ❏ no   ❏ sometimes   ❏ loud   ❏ soft   ❏ medium
❏ I use headphones

Do you mind your roommate listening to music when studying/in your room? *(check all that apply)*
❏ yes   ❏ no   ❏ sometimes   ❏ loud   ❏ soft   ❏ medium
❏ They need to wear headphones

Sample Roommate Questionnaire, continued

Neatness:

Please choose one of the following to describe yourself:
❏ clean   ❏ a little messy   ❏ extremely messy

What should your roommate know about your view of keeping a room clean?

_____

_____

_____

_____

_____

Personality:

Please choose one of the following to best describe yourself:
❏ outgoing   ❏ a little outgoing   ❏ reserved

Please choose one of the following to describe your ideal roommate:
❏ outgoing   ❏ a little outgoing   ❏ reserved   ❏ it doesn't matter

What are your hobbies/interests? _____

_____

_____

_____

_____

Bedtime and Wake-up:

I like to stay up late. ❏ yes ❏ no If yes, how late? _____

Does it depend on your class schedule? Explain. _____

_____

_____

_____

Sample Roommate Questionnaire, continued

I am generally: ❑ a light sleeper ❑ a heavy sleeper

Any sleeping habits we should know about? _____

_____

_____

_____

_____

Study Habits:

Do you think you will study in your room? *(check one)*
❑ yes   ❑ no   ❑ maybe

If yes, what times do you think you will study in your room?
(check all that apply)
❑ early mornings   ❑ weekday afternoons   ❑ weekday evenings
❑ late at night   ❑ weekends

Do you anticipate studying in your room with others? *(check one)*
❑ yes   ❑ no   ❑ maybe

Dorm Life:

Please check which statement best describes your thoughts about dorm life.
(check one)
❑ I want to have a room where everyone wants to hang out!
❑ I want to have a room where friends come by occasionally.
❑ I don't want other people spending time in my room.

Roommate changes or requests can be made after the first 3 weeks of the semester, but we cannot guarantee a room or roommate change.

5

![Academics banner]

Academics

Advocating for Academic Success

Since the early 1990s, when IDEA mandated increased student involvement in transition planning, promoting self-determination has been recognized as a best practice in the education of students with disabilities (Chambers et al., 2007). Self-determination is defined as a combination of skills, knowledge, and beliefs that enables a person to engage in goal-directed, self-regulated, autonomous behavior. An understanding of your strengths and limitations, together with a belief in yourself as a capable and effective learner, are essential to your self-determination and have a positive influence on improving your academic performance (Getzel & Thoma, 2008).

➤ Students who are self-determined are more likely to succeed at the college level, because they know what they want and how to get it. Hopefully, training in self-determination will begin during your public school years, so that you are better

 DOI: 10.4324/9781003233749-6

prepared to advocate for your needs at the college level. Once the semester begins, it is your responsibility to advocate for your needs both in and out of the classroom with the assistance of the Disability Services Coordinator. So, how does this responsibility apply to the classroom?

> For each of your courses, it is your responsibility to disclose your disability to the instructor. This typically includes providing the instructor with written documentation from the Disability Services Coordinator that confirms your disability and identifies the list of approved accommodations. You may want to schedule a brief meeting with your instructors to discuss the accommodations that have been approved by the university.

> Most instructors know that students with disabilities are protected under the law; however, they may not have the full knowledge of what that law entails. Nonetheless, college-level instructors are expected to possess the skills to provide instructional accommodations for students with disabilities (Eckes & Ochoa, 2005).

Academic Advising

Adjusting to the college environment is full of new challenges for all students, but for students with disabilities, the responsibility of managing academic coursework along with accommodations presents a unique set of challenges (Getzel & Thoma, 2008). Understanding and knowing what is required to meet your academic and personal needs is the first step to a successful college experience. As stated earlier, this process begins at freshman orientation when students typically have a scheduled meeting with their preassigned academic advisor. It is the advisor's role to assist students in planning their academic program. Often, this same advisor will assist you throughout your academic career.

In order to make the most of the initial meeting with the academic advisor, you will want to be familiar with the academic program you have chosen to pursue. Becoming familiar with the website and the university catalogue also will help you prepare questions that will need to be answered by the academic advisor.

Learning to Ask the Right Questions

1. Are you familiar with the university's website, and specifically, the information that discusses the program in which you are interested?
2. Do you have a copy of the university catalogue?
3. Do you know what paperwork you will need to bring for the meeting with your academic advisor?
4. Do you have a list of questions for your academic advisor?

Choosing Courses

Although the college experience can seem overwhelming for students with learning disabilities, adapting the traditional pacing for a course of study has proved to be an effective programming variable (McGuire & Shaw, 1987). A student taking two or three courses may be successful, but may not be able to handle a full course load. Many instructors expect students to spend at least one hour outside of class for every hour spent in class. That means a student taking 12 credit hours would spend at least 36 hours each week completing assignments and preparing for class. Even with accommodations, a student with a disability may need more time to complete assignments. Therefore, you may want to consider a reduced course load as well as evaluate the level of difficulty of the coursework you will be taking. Taymans (n.d.) offered strategies about becoming informed of the courses you should register for:

> **Participate in orientation programs.**
> These programs provide opportunities to become familiar with campus life and to ask questions of continuing students and advisors about classes, faculty, resources, and services.
> **Don't procrastinate.**
> Do not wait until the last minute to begin gathering information about courses and professors. Most Offices for Disability Support Services will allow students with disabilities to register a few days before other students.
> **Talk to other students.**
> Other students are an excellent source of information about classes and professors.
> **Audit classes.**
> It is possible to observe a class for a limited period of time to determine whether this is the right class. Students who audit a course are not responsible for exams or assignments.
> **Check the Internet.**
> Most colleges and universities offer an increasing amount of information, including the course syllabus (outline of the course), objectives, textbook, readings, and assignments.
> **Meet the professor.**
> Professors have scheduled office hours to answer questions about the course. Getting the textbooks and reading list ahead of time also allows students an opportunity to get a head start on the course. (Section 5)

If you have explored the curriculum, choose to take a reduced load, and are on financial aid, examine the financial aid criteria closely. Some forms of financial aid are dependent on the student taking 12 semester hours. This typically is the number of hours needed for an undergraduate student to be considered a full-time student.

Colleges and universities are not required to alter admissions requirements or make any changes to the program requirements for students with disabilities once they have been admitted. You should not assume that the college will waive or substitute certain courses once you are admitted. You can make requests, but it is up to the academic committee to make that decision. If it is decided that another course will meet the requirements of your degree plan, the committee may be willing to make the substitution or waiver. However, keep in mind that postsecondary institutions are not going to make any changes to a student's academic program that would lower the university's academic standards.

If you have made the decision to disclose your disability to the university in order to receive accommodations, you may want to discuss this information with your academic advisor as well, especially if the college has approved a reduced course load. This information may influence the way the advisor designs your course of study.

In addition, your parents will need to check with their insurance companies about course load requirements. Most insurance companies continue to cover full-time college students who are on their parents' insurance policy, but it is the decision of the insurance company to define what they consider to be a full-time student. When deciding on how many courses a student can successfully complete in one semester, the student needs to be aware of some of the differences in the academic environment between high school and college. Some of the differences may include:

> larger class sizes resulting in fewer opportunities to contact the instructor,
> higher level of difficulty in the content,
> more rigorous grading systems,
> higher expectation of independent work on assignments,
> longer class meeting times,
> extensive use of specific software programs to complete assignments,
> more emphasis placed on understanding theory,
> courses structured in a hybrid format (online and face to face) or solely through online instruction,
> fewer graded assignments contributing to a final grade, and
> more writing intensive assignments.

It is essential that you understand yourself as a learner when planning your course of study. You may want to refer to the Self-Advocacy Skills Worksheet you completed in Chapter 2 to assist you in choosing courses and making decisions about the course load. If you are worried about the transition to college regarding the adjustment to course load and learning the campus, you might enroll in a postsecondary summer preparatory program. These programs provide you with experiences that you are likely to engage in during your time in college. Some examples of this are living in the dorm and eating in dining halls. Many of the programs have a specific content area focus. The preparatory program may be a 3-week event that centers around English or science, technology, engineering, and math (STEM) subjects. Some grant-funded programs may offer incoming freshmen the opportunity to attend a preparatory program to assist them with improving study skills (U.S. Department of Education, n.d.-b).

Learning to Ask the Right Questions

1. How many courses can you successfully complete in a semester?
2. How much content can you read between class meetings? (Keep in mind that most courses meet every other day.)
3. How much writing can you complete between class meetings?
4. Do you have effective library skills?
5. Do you know how to use effectively use the Internet for academic research? Have you familiarized yourself with the technology/software necessary to complete assignments?

Scheduling

Will you be able to wake up and pay attention in an 8 a.m. class? This is an important consideration for all college students—especially those who have difficulties managing their time. In addition, some students with disabilities may be on medication that makes it difficult for them to attend an early morning class. Therefore, it may be better to schedule classes later in the day. The number of sections offered for a particular course will depend on the number of students needing to complete the course as part of their program of study.

Therefore, you may not always have a lot of options in scheduling courses. Many instructors may not take attendance, but you will still be held responsible for learning the information covered during each class and for completing assignments, projects, and exams on time.

In some cases, if a course is not offered at a time that is most beneficial to your learning or if a course fills up before you can register for it, you may want to put off taking the course until the next semester and replace it with another course needed to complete your degree plan. This is something you will want to discuss with your academic advisor because sometimes a particular course is a prerequisite for another course you will need to take. Your advisor can provide you more direction if this should be the case. However, you should keep in mind that there is some flexibility in the order in which you complete the courses required to graduate.

Course Requirements

Most instructors give a copy of the course syllabus to students on the first day of class, or they may post it online prior to the first class meeting. As soon as you get the syllabus, review the document and make a list of any questions you may have about the course. Some of these may include questions about the class format, requirements such as amount of reading and writing, types of exams given, and the instructor's teaching style. You may want to schedule a brief meeting with the instructor after the first class to address these questions early in the semester. This is an effective way to minimize the stress and misunderstandings that may occur between you and your instructor in regard to course requirements. You also may use this same meeting to disclose your disability, turn in a copy of the documentation to the instructor, and discuss how the accommodations will be implemented within that particular course.

The syllabus typically includes information about the required texts for the course. You can purchase textbooks a couple of weeks before the class begins, so you have a chance to read through some of the information you will be learning. Some students take advantage of this by reading slightly ahead of the course syllabus, starting in the summer, which allows a little more time for reading between class meetings. Several university bookstores allow students to preorder books by entering their class schedules. Students can order the textbooks based off their schedule, usually using an online program the bookstore has created. The schedule is accessed by the university bookstore, the instructors' book lists are checked, and the correct books are pulled, bagged, and ready for pick-up by the students. In most cases, you can specify if you want new or used books. All you have to do is go to the bookstore and pay for the books. This saves a lot of time and assures that you are purchasing the correct books. Keep in mind that some professors will ask for supplementary textbooks that are optional. You can wait to purchase these books until you receive additional information from your instructor. Preordering books is a great option for first-semester students, but you also should familiarize yourself with how the bookstore works so that you can pick up any materials (like those supplementary textbooks) later. One downside to preordering books is that some campuses have multiple bookstores, and some students prefer to shop around the stores for the best pricing and conditions of used books. But, for your first semester, preordering books is an excellent way to ensure you have what you need, when you need it.

Also, you can use the syllabus to develop a calendar plan for completing assignments and projects. You should carefully review the syllabus for any information that requires the use of specialized equipment or technology. For example, many universities utilize web-based server software programs to help facilitate instruction, often referred to as Learning Management Systems (LMS), such as Blackboard, Moodle, Brightspace, or Canvas. These programs are simply tools used to allow professors to post readings, assignment sheets, and syllabi. The LMS provides a place where PowerPoint, Captivate, video, audio, animation, and other applications can be uploaded to enhance student learning experiences. The LMS also allows professors to collect student work submitted online. If you are not familiar with these programs, you can participate in university-wide training sessions. Many institutions offer technology training sessions early in the semester and prior to the beginning of courses. Often these training sessions are conducted by university libraries, which teach library-specific technology, such as the use of the school catalogue and Internet databases, along with training on basic computer programs. However, you should already be well-versed in using software programs such as Microsoft Word, PowerPoint, and Excel. These programs are likely to be utilized quite often by your instructors. Course instructors typically do not provide training on software programs unless they are directly related to the course offering.

Preparing Academically

As previously mentioned, the role of the student drastically changes when moving from the high school setting to the college campus. This is particularly true with academic responsibilities. Although specific accommodations can be granted to students with disabilities, the university is not required to prepare students or to strengthen skills necessary to reduce the intensification of the academic workload. You should examine areas in which you can strengthen your academic skills. Getzel and Wehman (2005) provided examples of areas for strengthening academic skills. These particular skills can be addressed through attendance at workshops, during secondary education, or in the home environment prior to attending college. Most college campuses will offer mini-workshops or seminars to the general population of students to address the following areas:

> - writing strategies,
> - reading skills,
> - proofreading skills,
> - color-coding information and other organization skills,
> - mnemonics for memorization,
> - test-taking strategies,
> - managing time,
> - video feedback sessions,
> - role-playing exam questions or presentations, and
> - general study skills.

Contact the coordinator at the Student Disability Services Office for information regarding dates and offerings of any seminars and workshops offered on your campus. In addition, you should receive some instruction prior to entering college on those skills necessary to use a computer and/or specific assistive technology that you may be using or accessing through the SDSO.

Effective Use of Study Skills

For students with disabilities, the use of effective study skills is crucial in successfully completing an academic program. You will want to develop strategies to assist you in learning information that is presented in a variety of formats that may be different from those used in your high school classes. You need to understand your own learning style even though college classes are not always taught in the same way that students learn. You can refer to the Study Skills Checklist at the end of this chapter to help identify how you learn information.

When you understand how you learn and retain new information, you will be more successful in developing study skills that match your learning style. Also, time management in this digital world can be very challenging, but learning to manage your time lowers stress, while procrastination increases stress. The following is a list of tips you can use to manage not only your academic classes but also your time as you prepare for class.

Tips for Completing Reading Assignments

- Before the first class, buy the textbook.
- Scan the first chapter and look at the pictures, graphs, and headings.
- Write down unknown vocabulary words and look them up.
- Use sticky notes to identify key words or sections.
- Highlight important information in the chapter.
- Read in short time blocks.
- Keep up with assigned readings.

Tips for Completing Written Assignments

- Brainstorm ideas for your topic.
- Research your topic using the library's online databases.
- Use graphic organizers to help organize your thoughts and plan your paper or response to an assignment. (See https://my.hrw.com/nsmedia/intgos/html/igo.htm for interactive graphic organizers.)
- Use index cards to help organize the information.
- Go to the writing center for help (available at most colleges).

Tips for Note-Taking

- Determine the best method for note-taking: digital, hand-written, or a combination of both.
- Be prepared—have the necessary materials to take notes.

- ➤ Consider having a spiral notebook for each course so that all notes can be kept together.
- ➤ Use short phrases instead of complete sentences.
- ➤ Ask questions for clarification.
- ➤ Use abbreviations to reduce the amount of writing.
- ➤ Compare your notes with another student's.
- ➤ Use audio recordings. You will need to obtain the consent of the instructor unless it is in your approved accommodations.
- ➤ Get a copy of the instructor's notes. This may be in your approved accommodations.
- ➤ Use specific note-taking strategies.

Tips for Organization

- ➤ Keep an organized notebook for each course that includes the course syllabus and any guidelines or rubrics for assignments.
- ➤ Use color-coded folders to organize classwork and assignments.
- ➤ Create digital folders.
- ➤ Reduce excess materials in and on your desk.
- ➤ Label spaces.

Tips for Time Management

- ➤ Plan your day: Purchase a weekly planner/calendar or utilize the planner/calendar function on your mobile device.
- ➤ Record assignments, due dates, and exam schedules in your paper/digital planner.
- ➤ Schedule study times, reading sessions, and project work on a daily basis.
- ➤ Keep to a routine
- ➤ Divide assignments into smaller sections and set a due date for each section.
- ➤ Choose a location that is conducive to studying.

> ➤ Download and use a mobile app to help with prioritizing and scheduling, such as Clear.

Learning to Ask the Right Questions

1. Have you completed the Study Skills Checklist at the end of this chapter?
2. Do you have a weekly planner/calendar?
3. Do you have strategies in place to help you complete reading and writing assignments?
4. Do you have a note-taking system?

Accommodations in the Classroom

Under Section 504 of the Rehabilitation Act, institutions are required to make modifications in academic requirements as necessary to ensure that such requirements do not discriminate or have the effect of discriminating against a qualified applicant with disabilities (Sec. 104.44a). Based on this statement, reasonable accommodations are to be provided on a case-by-case basis dependent on the student's documentation. Academic accommodations have been defined as "practices and procedures in the areas of presentation, response, setting, and timing/scheduling that provide equitable access during instruction and assessment for students with disabilities" (Thompson et al., 2005, p. 17), but the responsibility of attaining accommodations in college is a two-way street (Scott, 1991). It is the responsibility of the college to provide the accommodation and the responsibility of the student to make a timely and reasonable request (Brinckerhoff et al., 2001). Although the roles and actions of students, faculty, and Disability Services Coordinators vary from institution to institution, some general processes include the following.

Role/Action of the Student

> Identify the office that provides accommodations for students with a disability.

> Register as a student with a disability (documentation will be requested, which may include medical, psychological, and/or educational documentation). It is a good idea to call or visit the website to determine what documentation you will need to have. This will allow you to gather the information prior to arriving at the office.

> Notify the Student Disability Services Office of your need for academic adjustments or accommodations.

> Actively engage in the conversation regarding the academic adjustments you need. This is a time when self-advocacy is critical. Share your past experiences of what has worked and what has not worked. The process of determining and implementing appropriate academic adjustments can be daunting if you are ill-prepared.

> You will be responsible for sharing a letter of accommodation (written by the SDSO coordinator) with your class instructors.

> Once your accommodations or academic adjustments have been put in place, it is your responsibility to notify the office when the adjustments are not working or when the accommodations are not being provided to you by the faculty member. Self-monitoring your success with the accommodations is essential.

Role/Action of the Disability Services Coordinator

> Will collect the required documentation to determine whether you are eligible for services. This includes determining if the disability falls in accordance with state and federal laws.

> The office may conduct an interview when you submit the determination documentation.

- Confidentially maintains/stores medical, educational, and/or psychological documentation.
- Works alongside you to identify what accommodations will be provided.
- Will provide you with a letter that indicates your accommodations. The letter of accommodations (LOA) is frequently use to notify your course instructors/faculty members of the specific accommodations you are to receive. If additional documentation is necessary to maintain eligibility or to change accommodations, the coordinator will request it.
- Serves as a venue to direct you to resources, policies, and processes for handling a dispute regarding your disability.

Role/Action of Faculty

- Refer student to SDSO if a student approaches them for accommodations who does not have a Letter of Accommodations (LOA).
- Provide private room for discussions with student regarding their disability or LOA.
- Provide and implement the accommodation(s) listed in the LOA.
- Arrange private testing space if indicated in LOA.
- Be open to communication with students to determine effectiveness of accommodations.
- Maintain confidentiality.
- Request assistance from the Disability Services Coordinator if experiencing difficulty with implementing the accommodations.
- Refer disputes to the Disability Services Coordinator.

Selecting Appropriate Accommodations

Determining which accommodations would benefit you is not a decision that should be made without critically analyzing your needs. The Student Disability Services Office will assist you in determining which accommodations will support you in the college setting. Students with disabilities may have challenges with auditory, visual, or tactile information. It may take longer for some students who have learning difficulties to process written information or to complete lengthy reading assignments, while others may have difficulties focusing on tasks, organizing their materials, or managing their time. For example, if you are a student who has a difficult time paying attention in class, but can complete the work successfully if you had all of the information shared in class, one or more of the following accommodations may benefit you:

> ➤ use of an audio recorder or assistive listening device,
> ➤ use of a note-taker (e.g., another student in the class),
> ➤ copy of the instructor's notes,
> ➤ permission to record lectures, and
> ➤ alternate testing environment (a separate room or a smaller group of students).

If you struggle to complete lengthy written assignments or essay exams because of difficulties with the writing process, or you become easily distracted, one or more of the following accommodations may benefit you:

> ➤ graphic organizer software,
> ➤ access to assistive technology devices,
> ➤ altered test formats (e.g., oral response, dictating),
> ➤ a quiet work location, and
> ➤ extra time on assignments and tests.

If reading and processing written language is a difficult task for you, one or more of the following accommodations need to be considered:

> a quiet work location,
> reduced length of reading assignments,
> extra time on assignments and tests, and
> audiobooks.

Although these lists do not include all of the accommodations that a student may request, understanding the characteristics of your disability and the areas that may be challenging for you as a college student will help in deciding on the accommodations that will provide the most benefits as you pursue a college degree.

In addition, other accommodations can be included in your program that may have a major impact on the success of your educational experience. For example, some colleges give specific timelines as to the length of time students are permitted to complete their degree (e.g., 4 years). This may not be a reasonable timeline for students who need to have a reduction in the course load each semester as an accommodation. Therefore, this would need to be negotiated at the beginning of your program. Also, because of a specific disability, you may need to request a substitution for a specific course that is considered a nonstandard substitution. Again, it would be up to the college to decide if this substitution would jeopardize the integrity of the program of study or be a reasonable accommodation in order to provide you with an equal opportunity to achieve equal results.

If a student makes a request for an accommodation that the college does not feel constitutes a "reasonable accommodation," the college can propose an alternative accommodation. Under Section 504, students with learning disabilities are entitled to "equivalent access" to the educational environment, but students need to be willing to work with the college in coming to a reasonable consensus. Furthermore, if the proposed accommodation does not pose an undue financial or administrative burden on the institution or result in fundamental alterations in program requirements, then the institution must ultimately bear the costs of the accommodation (Brinckerhoff et al., 2001).

Additional information on accommodations for college students can be found at Wrightslaw. See https://www.wrightslaw.com/info/sec504.college.accoms.brown.htm for legal information, as well as links to additional resources regarding accommodations and rights and responsibilities of the student and the college or university.

Learning to Ask the Right Questions

1. Do you know which classroom and testing accommodations you require?
2. Do the accommodations you are requesting directly impact your ability to learn?
3. Do you understand the process for requesting accommodations?
4. Have you arranged a meeting with your instructor to discuss your academic accommodations?

Discussing Accommodations With College Professors

Once you have met with the Disability Services Coordinator, you should determine how and when you will share your accommodations with your instructors. It is highly recommended that students with disabilities, including learning disabilities, schedule an appointment early on with their instructors. If a teaching assistant (TA) is used for the course, you should request that the TA be present at the meeting. During this meeting, you should share the determined accommodations with your instructor and offer the opportunity for the instructor to provide further input as to their expectations in the class. Do not begin the meeting by demanding accommodations. A clear plan for the meeting should be established, allowing you to introduce yourself, explain that you have a documented disability, and talk about how this disability might affect your performance in the class. Although instructors should be familiar with specific disabilities, this is not always the case. Identifying some of the common characteristics of the disability and how it impacts your ability to be successful in the classroom will provide the perfect opportunity to discuss the accommodations that were established with the Disability Services Coordinator and how such accommodations will allow you to overcome possible obstacles within the classroom.

Most importantly, you should take ownership of your responsibilities within the class. These responsibilities should be expressed to the instructor, as well, and should include taking necessary actions to schedule appointments with the instructor when you are having difficulty with content or assessments for the course. You should establish collegial relationships with your instructors early on so that you can feel more comfortable discussing any problems that may arise. In the college setting, you will take many courses, and this process should be repeated with each instructor. If you do not share your accommodations with the instructor early on, the instructor will not be prepared to provide the necessary accommodations. However, when you are up front and honest about your accommodation needs, most instructors are willing to go above and beyond providing the basic accommodations. For example, instructors who have students in the class who need copies of notes often will post notes to Blackboard prior to lectures. Some instructors may even offer suggestions to the student such as participating in study groups or tutorials.

Explaining Accommodations to Friends and Classmates

As in the high school setting, peers or other classmates may notice that a student is getting what is perceived as special privileges. This perception may lead to confrontations by a classmate. In this situation, it is best to be up front and honest. For example, if you are given the accommodation of sitting close to the front of the class-room and seem to have better access to the professor, you may have to explain that if you do not sit there, you will be easily distracted or unable to focus on the material presented. Typically, this is enough. Often this situation does not arise in the instructional setting but rather in study groups or when meeting with assigned partners. It is recommended that you carefully evaluate the situation and determine if you should disclose your disability to your study peers.

If you do choose to share your specific disability, you should be prepared to state not only how this might challenge you in the group situation, but also what benefits you can contribute to the group. For example, if your specific learning disability involves difficulty with written expression, you should explain to the group that this may not be the best task for you. However, you may have developed excellent skills using specific software programs and can contribute by assisting with the design or presentation of the materials. Sharing your strengths with classmates will help your peers to more openly accept you for what you have to offer, not what challenges may be imposed on the group.

Grievance Procedures

As stated earlier, most instructors know that students with disabilities are protected under the law, and that instructors are expected to provide instructional accommodations for their students (Eckes & Ochoa, 2005). However, in a situation where you do not feel that the accommodations are being implemented, you will need to contact the Disability Services Coordinator. Hopefully, the coordinator will be able to resolve the issue with the instructor. As a general rule, disability grievance should be handled internally in efforts to resolve the issue. However, if internal grievance procedures do not resolve your complaint, you should contact the U.S. Department of Education Office for Civil Rights and complete the process for filing a complaint (see https://www.ed.gov/about/offices/list/ocr/complaintprocess.html for more information). In many cases, complaints must be filed within 180 days of the alleged discrimination. If you determine that filing a claim is necessary, it is important to be prepared with appropriate documentation that proves the discrimination occurred.

Learning to Ask the Right Questions

1. Who is the person to contact at the university you are attending if you feel you are being discriminated against because of your disability?
2. Have you read through the grievance process outlined by the U.S. Department of Education Office for Civil Rights?
3. Have you met with the instructor and informed them that you feel your accommodations are not being met?

Conclusion

This chapter contains some of the most important information for you as a prospective college student pursuing a degree. As a student with a disability, you need to have an understanding of your strengths and limitations and be proactive in obtaining the necessary services that will assist you in meeting your academic needs. This means that you will have to make the decision whether or not to disclose your disability; however, if you needed academic supports while you were in high school, there is a good chance that you will need them in college as well. Because of the increased responsibilities that will be placed on you, having people who can support you within this new academic environment can be the defining factor for success.

There is much more to college than just signing up for courses. Knowing and understanding yourself as a learner will help you develop an educational plan along with the support of your academic advisor and the Student Disability Services Office. They will be able to assist you in identifying the most appropriate accommodations, knowing how to discuss those accommodations with your professors, and knowing what process to follow if those accommodations are not being implemented in all of your classes. Seeing yourself as a capable and effective learner and being willing to self-advocate for your academic needs are essential to your achievement.

Student Interviews

When were you assigned an academic advisor, and when was your first meeting?

James: I was assigned an advisor at the beginning of my freshman year, and I met with her well before classes began. I really wanted to be prepared and take the correct courses for my degree plan, so it was good to start early. An advisor is a very important mentor to any student, but especially those with disabilities. During the first meeting, we used a generic degree plan to develop a long-term outline of the courses I would take over the next 4 years. My advisor makes sure I follow my degree plan and informs me of the basic services that are available; however, she is not very familiar with the Student Disability Services Office, so she recommended I visit them to explain and request services based on my disability.

Jared: I was assigned an advisor on campus and was able to meet with him. He was a computer engineering professor so he was very familiar with the coursework I had to take.

Ricky: I was assigned an academic advisor right away, at the beginning of my first semester. It was part of the H.E.L.P. program to have an advisor, and we met to help pick out classes and discuss expectations and requirements.

What information did your advisor share during that first meeting?

James: She explained the importance of following your degree plan. She cautioned against dropping any courses because it wastes time and money. Because of this, it is very important to carefully select your degree plan and courses. Also, she explained a lot of additional information regarding the teaching program at SHSU, including any specific requirements and coursework that applied to my own program of study.

Angela: I don't remember exactly what we discussed at our first meeting, but I know we determined what classes I would need to take and discussed the course load decision.

Jared: The main thing that we discussed in our first meeting was options for classes in my major and what the core classes (required classes) were that I had to take.

Ricky: We discussed what classes transferred from my year of community college, what classes I would need to take, and recommendations on how many courses to take per semester. Along the way we always discussed staying on track to get my degree. We also discussed what the expectations were of me and what I would need to do to stay in the program.

How did you decide on the appropriate course load?

James: At first, I chose the minimum amount for full time, because I wanted to ease myself into the demands of college coursework. As I look back, it was a good choice because it enabled me to focus on adjusting to college life without being overwhelmed. My advice would be to take the least amount of hours you possibly can, while still progressing through your degree plan. One strategy I used was that I would take less hours in the fall and spring and make up the difference in the summer. The important point to remember is that you should make the decision based on what you are comfortable with.

Ricky: My advisors and tutors were very helpful in helping me navigate a course load I could handle. I think attending community college for a year helped ease me into a college level course of study. Because I was able to be tutored in any/all classes, I felt supported and less likely to feel alone if I had trouble understanding certain academic studies.

What process did you use in advocating for yourself in your courses?

James: I always try to communicate with my professors in a professional and honest manner regarding my needs and my disability. The process at my university is quite simple, and it takes very little time to request the accommodations. First, I visit the Student Disability Services Office and provide them with information regarding my diagnosis, as well as my impression of what I need to succeed at SHSU. Then the office prepares accommodations forms for each of my professors, which I have to deliver, explain, and return signed. If a professor has reasonable questions to ask me about my accommodations, I will do whatever I can to explain things and clarify my needs. The three key points to remember are: Be honest, be flexible, and be reasonable.

Jared: I built my schedule around the core coursework that was required and added in courses from my major based on what I wanted my schedule to look like. My schedule was based on my preferences and requirements. I took five courses my first semester.

Ricky: Because most of my tutors were students themselves, we could also be on a more relaxed level. I spent so much time in the H.E.L.P. Center that I got to know most everyone, including the ladies who worked administratively. It was a very mutually supportive atmosphere and one I found worked tremendously for me.

James: The most helpful thing any professor has done in regard to my accommodations is their willingness to openly discuss my disability and listen to my concerns. Sometimes they have even thought of better and more efficient ways to provide an accommodation. The professors are required to provide certain accommodations, but the list is not exhaustive and can be expanded upon or modified with your consent. For example, an accommodation I utilize frequently is the assistance of a volunteer student note-taker. After reading my form, my math professor offered to simply make copies of her lecture notes for me, in exchange for my attempt to do my best to take notes and use her notes only as a study tool. This arrangement worked very well for me and I expressed my appreciation to that professor at the end of the course.

Jared: Although it was not stated in my accommodations, I made it a point to get to know my professors and advisors during the semester. I utilize office hours of my professors/TA and also participate in study groups. I also go to the library and study with friends. I had a very successful first semester with a 4.0 GPA.

Ricky: If I needed help from a professor, I have always found honesty to be the best policy . . . being honest about what I needed help with and that I may have struggled with a certain concept of instruction. They were, for the most part, always willing to give me their time and extra help. As long as you're a student that always shows up, attends class, and puts forth an effort, most professors are willing to help.

Was there a particular type of teaching style that worked best for you?

Angela: Visual styles, as well as group work, seem to work best for me, because I need to be able to see things in order to understand them. For instance, lectures are very hard for me because I cannot process what the professor is saying in order to take notes. Also, when I am able to picture something I can understand it.

Jared: I prefer to learn from seeing examples, and I am a hands-on learner. I take notes, make note cards to study, and reread all of my materials and notes. I do ask questions to clarify if I do not understand the content or discussions.

Ricky: I always struggled with straight lecture style of teaching. I found it hard to keep up writing notes and focused so much on that, I would often miss parts of the lecture. I worked better if professors provided visuals with a hands-on style, and if we worked in a small group setting. Small classroom size makes a difference for me too, as I felt it was a more cohesive group and more personable.

Study Skills Checklist

	Yes	No	Somewhat
Do I know how to manage my time?	❏	❏	❏
Do I know how to use a planner—either a digital version or hard copy?	❏	❏	❏
Do I know how to conduct research in a library with hard copy texts?	❏	❏	❏
Do I know how to use the library's online resources?	❏	❏	❏
Do I know how and when to seek tutoring services on campus?	❏	❏	❏
Can I take notes from a class lecture in a written format?	❏	❏	❏
Can I take class notes on a computer?	❏	❏	❏
Can I take notes from an audio recording?	❏	❏	❏
Can I access my textbooks as audiobooks?	❏	❏	❏
Do I know how to take notes from an online course?	❏	❏	❏
Do I know how to highlight important information in my reading assignments?	❏	❏	❏
Do I know how to study for different kinds of tests?	❏	❏	❏
Do I know how to take different kinds of tests (written and digital)?	❏	❏	❏

Study Skills Checklist, continued

	Yes	No	Somewhat
Do I need extra time for tests?	❏	❏	❏
Am I usually prepared for class (e.g., notebook, text-book, computer, pen)?	❏	❏	❏
Am I usually on time for class?	❏	❏	❏
Do I skip classes often?	❏	❏	❏
Is my schoolwork organized for each course (e.g., folders, computer files, handwritten or digital notes)?	❏	❏	❏
Are my assignments completed on time?	❏	❏	❏
Is my behavior in class appropriate and not distracting to others?	❏	❏	❏
Do I stay focused in class?	❏	❏	❏
Can I do my share of a group project?	❏	❏	❏
Am I willing to discuss any accommodations I may need with my professors (if I have a 504 plan in place)?	❏	❏	❏

6

Adapting to University Life

Few people would argue that the college experience involves just attending classes. Just ask any college student. Students are only in class for a small amount of time each week, and part of the college experience is being able to explore interests beyond academics. Most postsecondary institutions provide students with a wealth of information, from academics to student life, on their website. This information may have played a role in helping students choose the college or university that seemed to be the best fit. Once classes start, you will want to explore opportunities in which you can pursue your own interests.

Exploring Campus Life

Attending freshman orientation is a good first step to discover ways to get involved in campus life, but you have to make the first

 DOI: 10.4324/9781003233749-7

move in actually getting involved. Most campuses have a campus life or student affairs office that will provide detailed information on all of the activities and organizations offered at the university. These offices often host websites that include a listing of the contact information for organizations along with possible meeting dates and times. Many organizations also advertise new member meetings or information sessions on bulletin boards across campus. You can use lists of organizations and advertisements as sources to determine what opportunities are available to you. Then, it is up to you to take the next step.

Typically, universities offer a wide array of activities for students to become involved in. Many clubs or organizations have a specific focus such as:

> service,
> specific interest areas/hobbies,
> academics,
> cultural activities,
> social interaction (fraternities or sororities),
> religion,
> honors programming (honor societies), and
> student governance (student body officers, student courts).

Obviously, the names of specific organizations will vary from campus to campus. However, organizations like Habitat for Humanity (service-based), National FFA Organization (interest-based), Golden Key International Honour Society (honors-based), and Young Life (religious) are national organizations with college chapters. Some universities also house local organizations particular to each university or to a region or consortium of universities. No matter what you choose, every university has myriad opportunities available for student involvement.

With so many opportunities available, you will have to make some choices regarding how many activities and organizations you can join. You need to be cautious about becoming too involved before knowing how much free time you will have in your academic schedule. Each semester, you will want to reevaluate your level of involvement. Often, students with disabilities find that some semesters require them to limit the amount of time they are involved in extracurricular activities, while other semesters may allow more time for involvement. Keep in mind that some universities limit student involvement during the first semester; for example, some schools do not allow first-semester students to join time-intensive sororities and fraternities.

Active participation in campus life is an important part of the postsecondary experience and also may help you avoid the isolation that can occur, especially if it is your first time living away from your home. Extracurricular activities also provide you with opportunities to connect with other students who have similar interests.

Athletics

Many students with disabilities are actively involved in organized sports on campus. Specific accommodations for student-athletes with disabilities are available, and the National Collegiate Athletic Association (NCAA) has increased efforts to be inclusive in its policies and practices. This is the statement directly from the NCAA (n.d.):

> The NCAA encourages participation by student-athletes with disabilities (physical or mental) in intercollegiate athletics and physical activities to the full extent of their interests and abilities. An NCAA member institution will have the right to seek, on behalf of any student-athlete with a disability participating on the member's team, a reasonable modification or accommodation of a playing rule, provided that the modification or accommodation would not:
> > ➤ Compromise the safety of, or increase the risk of injury to, any other student-athlete;

> ➤ Change an essential element that would fundamentally al her competitors. (para. 3)

If you are a student participating in athletics, make sure you meet with the athletic director and/or liaison to clearly understand the accommodations available to you. Several colleges have liaisons that facilitate academic support services for athletes, including those with disabilities. For example, tutoring programs and mentorships are often available to athletes. Students who access these services report higher levels of success in balancing academic work and athletics.

Time Management

Managing one's time can be a difficult task for any college student. This holds especially true for students with identified disabilities. Finding a healthy balance between academics and activities is essential in a successful college experience. You need to schedule a specific time each day for studying. The designated time should be chosen based on when you are the most alert. This time may vary each day depending on your class schedule. You also should study your most difficult or least favorite subject first. Studying for the most difficult subject first will allow you greater opportunity to focus. Students who have difficulty maintaining focus may need to take frequent breaks during studying.

Using a planner will help you keep up with your assignments. Many students begin each semester by setting up a detailed schedule that is too difficult to follow and give up the scheduling idea completely. You can establish a daily, weekly, and semester-long schedule using an academic planner. Many students utilize the applications and calendars on their phones in lieu of a physical planner. Academic planners and calendar applications allow students to see the entire semester at a glance and know that some activities are fixed and will not be changed. At the same time, seeing the entire semester at a glance can sometimes be overwhelming in regard to how much has to be accomplished before the semester ends, so approaching the semester one week at a time gives you a little more control. However, in order to effectively manage your time, you must organize your time on a daily basis that fits into your weeklong plan. Many cell phones have built-in notification systems that can be used to remind you of upcoming events, exams, due dates, and activities. The following example is a method of organizing time that has been helpful to many students with and without disabilities.

1. **Long-term schedule:** At the beginning of the semester, write in your fixed schedule. This includes classes, job hours, organization meetings, and other regular commitments.

2. **Weekly schedule:** On Sunday evening each week, write in all of the assignments that you need to complete or work on and any nonacademic activities you plan to attend. These will change each week, so this will need to be completed each Sunday evening. For example:
   - Club meeting Monday night
   - Read Chapter 9 in history by Wednesday
   - Develop outline for math project by Thursday
   - English quiz on Friday

3. **Daily schedule:** Before going to bed each evening, create a specific daily schedule for the following day. Enter what has to be completed, and don't forget to add in study time. A daily schedule might include:
   - 9:00–9:45 a.m.: Review for English quiz
   - 2:00–3:30 p.m.: Read Chapter 9 in history
   - 3:45–5:00 p.m.: Library—work on math project
   - 7:30–9:30 p.m.: Organizational meeting
   - 11:00–11:15 p.m.: Review rest of week and fill in tomorrow's schedule

Some additional examples of a weekly and monthly calendar/planner can be found at the end of the chapter.

Developing Good Study Habits

Another part of time management is deciding where to study. You must first determine what kind of setting is most conducive to your personal study habits. For example, a student with ADHD may need a quiet environment with no distractions. If this is the case, then the dormitory is probably not an option. Another consideration is whether or not you have a computer in your dorm room. If a computer is not available, you may need to study in a computer lab setting. The environment you choose to study in may vary across courses. However, you will need to be able to self-monitor the effectiveness of each setting you choose.

Many students with ADHD or learning disabilities have indicated that it is helpful to participate in study groups, while some students with ASD may have difficulty working in this situation. Working in small groups involves a vast array of social skills. Study groups can be helpful in allowing students to discuss and clarify concepts that have been covered in class. Typically, study groups are developed through an informal process of asking other students in the class if they are interested in getting together outside of class to cover the material. For some students, the opportunity to talk about the content can be an effective strategy for learning and reinforcing new material, although some students with disabilities find it difficult to make connections with peers in the classroom setting. Students should check with the professor to determine if they are aware of a study group taking place.

Often, the office of student services or the counseling center will offer specific instruction in critical elements such as working as a team member, active and critical listening skills, accepting constructive feedback, managing time, understanding expectations of the team, and forming friendships. In addition, students without disabilities in the group may not clearly understand your limitations or specific disabilities. Most college students with disabilities whom we interviewed felt strongly that in order to successfully participate in small groups, they needed to disclose and explain their disability to their peers. During the explanation, students were able to not only identify their limitations, but also discuss how their particular strengths would benefit the group.

In addition to participation in study groups, keeping up with the assigned readings and assignments is essential to managing time. Even the most effective study plan is not going to work if you do not follow through. It is difficult for most students to play catch-up if they start falling behind. This is especially true for students with disabilities. If you develop a plan that provides a balance between academics and activities, you are less likely to feel overwhelmed and more likely to have a successful semester. Many postsecondary institutions provide services that assist students in time management.

Learning to Ask the Right Questions

1. Do you know what activities or organizations you would like to be involved in? How much time would your participation take?
2. Are you good at managing your time?
3. Do you know how to use a planner for daily, weekly, and long-term assignments?
4. Do you know how to schedule time for academic tasks while leaving time for extracurricular activities?
5. What type of setting is most conducive to your study habits?
6. What social skills are necessary to participate in a study group?

Social Issues

Although the focus of college is academics, college is also about personal growth and discovery. Making new friends and engaging in social activities are important parts of campus life and the college experience. There are many new social challenges facing college students, no matter their social skills abilities or disabilities. With the frequent changing of class schedules, living situations, and long semester breaks, there is minimal consistency in remaining with the same group of people for any length of time. Yet, a key factor in making friends is spending time together. Planning activities with friends also will be a part of managing your time. Again, you have to find the balance between academics and social life. Students with social deficits may find this aspect of the college experience extremely difficult.

Understanding the effects of your disability and how it plays into your social interactions will better prepare you to adjust to the new social environment: "Reading and understanding cultural rules is necessary to life beyond college while understanding more subtle social cues and being able to manage one's impulses to act appropriately can be the fine line between fitting in or being isolated" (Quinn et al., 2000, p. 114). Because of the novelty of being on a college campus and all of the freedom that offers, students need to make a conscious effort in choosing friends. By attending campus activities, you can identify with other students who have similar interests. This also will allow you to fill unstructured time with university-approved activities. Students with disabilities who suffer from depression may struggle with downtime. Students who have too much free time may find themselves becoming involved with students who participate in questionable activities.

One of the most important social situations that you will be faced with is the possibility of living with a roommate. This can be challenging for any student, but it can be especially daunting for a student who has a disability that is characterized by social deficits. It will be up to you to decide whether or not you want to disclose the disability to your roommate, but it may make for an easier adjustment if your roommate has a basic understanding of your disability and how it may affect your social skill (see Chapter 4 for more).

You also will be interacting daily with people who are placed in various roles of authority, including professors, dorm staff, and other campus personnel across the college community. Because of the new social environment, social skills training needs to be a part of the transition plan while you are still in high school. This will provide an opportunity for you to role-play some of the social situations that will occur once you are living on a college campus (see Chapter 2). If you find yourself struggling with social issues or any other personal issues, most colleges provide counseling services that can offer assistance.

Counseling Services

The majority of college campuses offer counseling services that are staffed by professionals and provide most services free of charge. Prior to entering college, you should know what assistance is available to you and that you are not alone in learning to adapt to your new environment. Some stress will be expected as you adjust to your new life, but you may need additional support from the counseling office to understand how to best cope with these changes. A complete change in routine, lifestyle, and eating and sleeping habits, as well as isolation from family and old friends, can be overwhelming for all students, but it can be especially difficult for students with disabilities who may have had a number of supports in place before heading off to college. You can contact the university counseling office directly to discuss what type of assistance it provides. Some healthy stress management techniques for all college students include:

> - getting plenty of sleep,
> - sticking to your weekly planner,
> - exercising on a regular basis,
> - listening to your body,
> - eating a healthy diet, and
> - having healthy relationships.

Engaging in good health practices and setting healthy boundaries are effective means of stress prevention. Dealing with stress in a constructive way will enable you to have a more balanced, healthy, and productive college experience.

Learning to Ask the Right Questions

1. How do you choose your friends?
2. Do you know how to interact with people in authority?
3. Does the Student Disability Services Office offer support services directly related to social acceptance?
4. Does the Student Disability Services Office offer specific activities that involve the opportunity to interact with other individuals with disabilities similar to your own?
5. Do you know how to identify the causes of your stress?
6. Do you know what stress management techniques work best for you?

Conclusion

As any college student will attest, academics are only part of the college experience. You will be making new friends and pursuing other areas of interest outside of academia. College can be a lonely time for first-semester freshmen, as they often are living away from home for the first time. Fortunately, you can go to the campus life or student affairs office to explore the many opportunities that are available, but you have to find a balance between school work and your social life.

For college students in general, time management can be challenging. Developing a time management system, which should involve some type of planner or calendar, will be essential in helping you manage your time. However, this plan will not work unless you follow through. It can become very easy to spend your time with new friends and push academics aside. At the same time, you can become overwhelmed with trying to manage your new life and may need some additional assistance. Most colleges provide counseling services that can assist students in adapting to their new environment. College is about personal growth and discovery, and asking for additional support can be a healthy response to this new college experience.

Student Interviews

James: I found information about campus activities through two different sources. The first was through my professors in the College of Education. They provided information about different education-related organizations by having representatives visit our classes and by giving us literature on them. The other way I learned about activities and organizations was through the Student Activities Department, which serves as a resource on all campus activities and student organizations. They provide a campus calendar at the beginning of every semester, and they also maintain an active listing of all organizations and their contact information. Because my university has so many organizations, it is very useful to have a way to filter through all of the information. In addition, my university hosts several events each semester that feature different campus organization booths that disseminate information.

Ricky: I mostly learned about activities and organizations through my classmates and new friends. Sometimes there were flyers around the hallways of dorms and classrooms, and the student newspapers were also a source.

James: I primarily chose organizations that were related to my major, but I also became involved in honor societies and civic organizations. The organizations related to my degree were great because they taught me very useful information for my future classroom and connected me to my colleagues in other education classes. Based on my personal commitment to academic excellence, I chose to be involved with honor societies to find ways to get involved with other leaders and to demonstrate my commitment. The biggest piece of advice I could give would be to pick organizations that you know you will enjoy and to remember that if you begin to see an organization as an obligation instead of a personal commitment, it is time to move on. An organization is meant to enhance your college experience, not make it more difficult or stressful.

Jared: I have not chosen an organization to belong to yet but might be interested in football later. I have made several friends. I go to the gym daily. I attend events on campus. I have come out of my shell and put myself out there, and it has paid off. I have my first girlfriend and met a great group of guys I hang out with. It is a much better experience for me than high school.

Ricky: I joined a fraternity and played intramural lacrosse. I limited what I chose to participate in because I didn't want to overload my schedule and feel my time was going to be divided into too many places. I knew my priority was to study and get through my studies, but it's also important to find time to relax, have fun, and make friends.

Were you involved in campus life activities and organizations?

Angela: I attended Texas State Teacher Association and Sam Houston Council for Exceptional Children meetings. I attended a lot of sports events and made a lot of friends. I wanted to be involved in activities where there would be people who had the same interests as I do, and I also wanted to learn more about my degree and topics related to my interests.

Jared: I attend football games, basketball games, and am looking forward to attending a baseball game. I play pickup basketball with friends along with some touch football.

Ricky: I was asked by the H.E.L.P. program to speak to civic and parent groups about their program and my specific struggles and learning disabilities. It was an opportunity to share what the H.E.L.P. program had to offer and to let parents and students know that there are resources to facilitate a college experience. Sometimes having a learning disability can be isolating—causing the student to feel alone and that they're the only one struggling. Speaking to parents and students, I think, helped them see that everyone has something they struggle with and that there are resources out there to help.

What has been the most helpful in finding a balance between academics and activities?

James: At first, they were very difficult to balance, but I was determined to make it work. The best method I found to find a balance was using a schedule planner. I would input all of the days and times of my organization meetings and events and look for conflicts between my classes. Sometimes, I had to accept that I couldn't go to a certain event or meeting because class should and must come first, but I would try to make it up in some way. For instance, if I missed one meeting, I would make certain that I was at the next one. One important point I would stress is that you should remember the quality of your involvement is much more important than the quantity. It is better to be an active and dedicated member of one or two organizations than an inactive member of several.

Jared: I am very good at prioritizing and making a checklist of things to do.

Ricky: I think just knowing what you can and can't handle is the best tool. I didn't want too many activities, but I also wanted to have some fun outside the classroom. I was there to get my degree, and so that was my priority. I chose activities that wouldn't demand too much time away from study time. I think time management is probably one of the most difficult challenges, especially because your parents are not there to keep you on track.

How did you go about keeping a schedule of your daily, weekly, and semester-long activities?

James: I rely heavily on a day planner to enable me to keep my schedule on track and current. If I write something in my planner, I am guaranteed to be there; if I don't remember to do this, I will simply forget, even if it's only a day later. I learned this skill in high school, and I have found it to be a lifesaver. I have accepted that I am very forgetful; however, I have learned to use my planner as an effective means of compensation for this. The main point is to use the method that works best for you, whether that be digital or hardcopies. If you are unsure of what method to use, ask for help from a teacher or a counselor.

Angela: I religiously use a day planner, and I always have multiple to-do and reminder lists going at all times. I tried to stay on top of my academics so that when the activities I wanted to participate in came up, I was able to take advantage of the opportunities and have fun instead of having to turn things down.

Ricky: I kept a planner, and the H.E.L.P. tutors were very good at making sure you were keeping on track with studying, turning in projects, and attending class.

How did you go about developing friendships?

James: The most beneficial avenue for being successful in developing friendships was through my participation in organizations. The organizations provided a relaxed atmosphere for meeting people and socializing. I found this forum to be extremely helpful in developing friendly relationships during my freshman year. Once I became an officer in several of these organizations, they provided me with even more opportunities to make friends. I also met other people through networking with existing friends. Everyone is connected through different people and many of the friends I made were met through the friends of other friends. The best way to develop solid and lasting friendships is simply to be cordial and be willing to take risks, even if it's outside of your comfort zone. Go to a party, attend a football game, or go to a social dinner—all of these activities can lead to making more friends and opening up brand-new opportunities for friendship.

Angela: I already had a couple friends who attended college before I got there, so I met their friends and also made friends of my own. I also met a lot of people who were taking the same classes.

Ricky: I never had a problem making friends, so just being involved in dorm life and activities and networking with other friends—it was easy making friends.

Sample Monthly Calendar/Planner
September

Sunday	Monday	Tuesday	Wednesday	Thursday	Friday	Saturday
				1 Math Project Due 2–4 Library	**2**	**3**
4	**5** 6–8 Study Group	**6**	**7**	**8** 2–4 Library	**9**	**10** Home for the Weekend
11 Home for the Weekend	**12** 6–8 Study Group	**13**	**14** Science Exam	**15** 2–4 Library	**16**	**17**
18	**19** 6–8 Study Group	**20**	**21**	**22** 2–4 Library	**23**	**24** Community Project
25	**26** 6–8 Study Group	**27**	**28**	**29** 2–4 Library	**30**	**31**

Sample Weekly Planner

Week of Sept. 1–7						
	CHEM 3301	ENG 1301	BIO 3311	GOV 3310	Study Time	Other Activities
Monday	8–9 a.m.		12–3 p.m.		7–9 p.m.	
Tuesday		11–1 p.m.		3–5 p.m.	8–10 p.m.	
Wednesday	8–9 a.m.		12–3 p.m.		7–9 p.m.	
Thursday		11–1 p.m.			8–10 p.m.	6–7 p.m. Drama Team Mtg.
Friday	Library (a.m.)			Free Time		Home for Weekend

Student should fill in academic assignments and extracurricular activities on their weekly calendar.

7

Family and College Success

College counselors, professors, and advisors often find that students and their parents/guardians have a different view or perspective of the college process, including how they will go about transitioning into college life. For some families, the parent/guardian may feel strongly about their child attending college, while the student feels less prepared. Other times, the feelings are reversed, with the student feeling more prepared and independent as the parent struggles to accept that their child has moved to the next stage in life. The conversation about fears, excitement, and level of preparedness is often buried under the to-do list of the college process. All families should take time to determine if the student and the parent have the same views, opinions, and expectations, and if not, make sure the expectations for the process are agreed upon. It is unfortunate when expectations are not defined, and one or all parties involved experience discouragement or disappointment. Keeping lines of communication open during the process and respecting each other's options

 DOI: 10.4324/9781003233749-8

proves essential when tough decisions are to be made. This includes thinking ahead and being open to changes.

One of the most common situations that families struggle with is when students are not accepted into the college of their choice. Often parents and students have not discussed the possibility of another college or a community or junior college as an option. Many times what is perceived as a setback can lead to an ultimately better situation. For example, during an interview, Ricky's parents shared that even though Ricky was disappointed that he wasn't accepted into his first choice of colleges, the outcome proved to be successful for all of them:

> We always wanted Ricky to be able to have a college experience if that is what he wished for. We did not want his disability to hold him back or cause him to hesitate to apply and attend college. Our two older daughters had attended 4-year colleges away from home, and both had wonderful experiences—making new friends, learning to make decisions on their own, and time management. We always encouraged that mentality and never felt that his disability should or could hold him back—it may be a challenge but nothing he couldn't face head on.
>
> After he didn't get into his first choice of colleges, we decided together that going to the local community college for a year or two might be a good choice because he could be introduced to college-level classes and remain at home for study support. Plus, he could transfer to a 4-year college if he wished. During that first year of community college he heard about Marshall University from a family friend. In addition, a coworker of mine had a daughter with a learning disability and had attended Marshall University. He talked about their special program specifically designed for students' special classroom challenges. We researched

it, visited the school, and applied. It was truly the best situation and one we found to have a perfect support system. The program is called H.E.L.P., which stands for Higher Education for Learning Problems. It's a fee-based comprehensive academic support program. They have their own building, with study rooms, resources, and tutors. Ricky had tutors for as many subjects as he felt he needed, and he reported there every day for study. The tutors, in turn, then reported to us every semester on his progress—such as his accomplishments, his strengths, and things he needed to improve. He had multiple accommodations, including being able to take his tests in their study rooms and help with scheduling classes and staying on track with his degree program. He attended every session and felt very supported and totally committed to taking advantage of this wonderful resource. As parents, this was a great relief because he had been receiving a lot of support at home. We thought his college experience was wonderful and everything we hoped for his success. The support system and resources at the H.E.L.P. program were phenomenal. The director often asked Ricky to speak to groups of parents and students about the program and his own academic struggles and challenges. He enjoyed a full and fun social life—making friends and participating in sports and other activities.

It is clear that Ricky and his family were open to a different pathway for Ricky's education, and Ricky's dream of becoming a teacher was achieved. For the past 5 years Ricky has been teaching students with learning disabilities at a local high school and coaching wrestling. His parents shared that they feel very fortunate to have found the H.E.L.P. program and very proud that Ricky was so committed to his own success. In other situations, a plan for a student may not go as expected, but with open communication and a willingness to change course and adapt, it is possible to graduate from college and pursue a desired career.

Family Perspectives

Throughout this book you may have noticed that the role of the parent often decreases as students move closer to entering college life. Parents sometimes feel discouraged or conflicted as you establish a more independent lifestyle. However, there are important roles that families play in helping you along your journey. Figure 5 provides an overview of some things parents can do to support you.

In the following sections, Ann and Mark shared their experiences as a mother and son progressing through the college process. Each section was written by Ann and Mark respectively. Mark was identified as a student with high-functioning ASD in sixth grade.

My Son Is a College Student! *by Ann*

My husband and I always knew our son was college bound. He had the academic ability necessary to attend college, and he had long had a track of study he was interested in—computer science. So where's the issue? Let's back up a little. Mark was a public school student for the entirety of K–12. He was diagnosed by the school as high-functioning ASD after sixth grade. The diagnosis was a good thing for him and for us because it required the school to work with him and support him. It gave our family ways to begin to support him as he tapped into his strengths and learned skills for things he (and we) wanted shored up. Fast forward to his senior year of high school in 2014.

As he was looking at colleges, I was looking at the kinds of supports available to him by the schools he was interested in attending. I found was that the schools he was interested in, although large insti-

Figure 5
Parents' Role in Supporting Students
During the College Transition

Some things for parents to keep in mind include the following:
» Getting into a brand-name school does not improve one's life. Teaching and learning are often better in schools you've never heard of.
» Be a "guide on the side," gently encouraging your child, rather than an all-knowing "sage on the stage." Be ready and able to demonstrate an understanding of the pressures these students are experiencing. Provide support.
» Know the critical skills your child needs to make major decisions.
» Understand how your child defines the important characteristics of their ideal college.
» Help your child find specific institutions that meet their individual needs.
» Set clear and realistic goals that reduce the pressure on your child and keep things in perspective.
» Think of yourself as a shepherd. Your job is to guide and protect. Some parents avoid interfering by withdrawing. Some parents are overbearing. Neither extreme is useful.
» Discuss college openly, gearing conversation toward what your son or daughter needs from a college and why—city or country environment, emphasis on Greek life, sports, student/faculty ratio, class size, special programs, etc.
» Listen to your child. Pay particular attention to what attracts them to certain schools.
» *Do not* complete applications, correct essays, or call colleges for information for your child. When a student has questions, an admissions office would prefer to hear from the student.
» *Do* keep track of dates, such as those for standardized tests, admissions deadlines, financial aid deadlines, and so forth. Adolescents experience considerable pressure during their last 2 years in high school. Often, they need someone else to keep track of some of the details, especially due dates.

Figure 5, continued

Some things for parents to keep in mind include the following:
» *Do* make copies of all applications because it's almost inevitable that a big typo will crawl onto the page and it will need to be redone. Proofread everything for errors, but do not make major changes.
» Discuss any limitations, such as cost, up front. Find out all you can about financial aid. If money is a problem, as it is for most people, discuss it rationally and explain that the family will need to take advantage of available scholarships, loans, or any other source of funds. But don't restrict your child's choices based solely on cost, because some colleges provide financial aid to all of their students.
» The college planning process is part of a life development process in which there are no right answers. The process is different for every person because the goal is to make a match between your child's strengths and interests and college offerings. The college that is perfect for someone you know may be totally wrong for your child. Let your student make their final decisions and own the process.
» The college search is like an arranged marriage. Make the best match you can—love will come later.

Note. Adapted from *College Planning for Gifted Students: Choosing and Getting Into the Right College* (Updated ed., pp. 9–10), by S. L. Berger, 2014, Taylor & Francis. Copyright 2014 by Taylor & Francis. Adapted with permission.

tutions, really didn't have a program designed to specifically support students on the spectrum. They had academic supports, which are certainly important, but not support for soft skills, like advocating for himself or knowing how to handle roommate problems, talk to a professor, or feel part of the student body. However, we thought he would be OK—he'd have to work harder in these areas and rely on us more. We toured, and he was accepted at all of the schools he applied to. One of the schools he was really interested in is a major university in Texas with satellite campuses throughout the state. The university wanted him to attend a particular satellite campus for the first year. Mark has a lot of self-awareness and took this offer off the table. His reasoning was that by the time he got to the main campus the next year, his sophomore year, the freshmen would have made friends and groups, and it would be difficult to make friends or become part of groups. His reasoning had nothing to do with others but, rather, with himself and the difficulty he had in social situations. I should also say at this point that we have an agreement with Mark that we expected him to take the number of courses per semester that he and his academic advisor felt he could handle with the understanding that should he not take a full load, he would go to summer school to make up those hours so that he would end each year with approximately 30 credit hours. That plan worked really well for him because it allowed him to tailor the college academic experience to meet his needs rather than him having to meet the school's expectations for the number of classes he'd need to take as he did in high school.

Before he had these acceptances, a friend recommended we attend Family to Family Network's (F2F) annual conference. F2F is a nonprofit in the Houston area that connects families that have a child with a disability to resources in the community. We were utilizing F2F services and had been introduced to the organization by a friend. I've since come to realize it is an outstanding and worthwhile organization.

One of the presentations on the agenda was a college panel staffed by members of the University of Houston's Office of Disability Services, Houston Community College Vocation Assessment and Skills Training (VAST) Academy, and Texas Tech's Connections for Academic Success and Employment (CASE) program. As Mark and I listened to the presentations and discussion, we realized that the University of Houston and Houston Community College programs would not be able to meet his needs in the way he needed them to be met.

Texas Tech's CASE program was different. At the time it was a grant-funded program through the Texas Department of Disability and Rehabilitative Services (now a division of the Texas Workforce

Commission). The program was headed by Dr. DeAnn Lechtenberger and is part of the Burkhart Center for Autism Education and Research at Texas Tech. CASE assists students who are college able and have autism and other developmental disabilities navigate college and empowers them to reach their postsecondary academic goals and find competitive employment after graduation. Mark knew this was a program worth exploring and introduced himself to Dr. Lechtenberger. He applied to Texas Tech and the CASE program. We were all thrilled and nervous when he was accepted. It takes a lot of letting go for a parent to have their child leave the nest and go to school so far away. Texas Tech in Lubbock is a 500-mile drive from Houston. What he got out of attending Texas Tech and being part of CASE is truly priceless.

Texas Tech is a wonderfully student-centric campus. From our perspective as parents, Texas Tech is a school highly interested in student success, and to that end, they have many programs in place for the general student population that help ensure student success. From the outside looking in, the disability services department works closely with students receiving services and on campus entities like the Burkhart Center.

Here's what Mark says about the CASE staff members: "They didn't look at me and say, he's a boy so he has these needs, or he's on the spectrum so he has these needs. Rather they looked at me and said, what does Mark need?" As his needs or goals changed, so did his program. That would be the best way to summarize this program. CASE looks at each student and, with the student's help, figures out what their needs and goals are and then develops a plan to meet those goals academically and otherwise. Each student begins their time in CASE by completing Birkman Method Assessment (see https://birkman.com/the-birkman-method), and then the results of that are part of the Wraparound Planning Process used to build an individualized plan. The support network provided by CASE pairs each student with a Learning Specialist who provides mentoring and navigational support. This relationship helped Mark throughout his time at school and in ways that are more than just the academic. Mark's Learning Specialist helped him prepare for life in school and after graduation. The wraparound team was made up with anyone Mark wanted on it. Beyond staff from the program, he was free to select whoever else he wanted on his team. This could have been us (his parents), a mentor he still worked with in Houston, or anyone he wanted to have. Because CASE was grant-funded at the time he was going through it, his wraparound team also included his Department of Assistive and Rehabilitative Services representative in Lubbock. That is not the case now unless someone is working with Texas Workforce Commission.

> The *wraparound process* is an intensive, individualized care planning and management process for children and adolescents with complex mental health and/or other needs (Bruns & Walker, 2010, p. 1). Although Ann and Mark worked with outside agencies, the agencies they utilized were more specific to Texas. Each state or region has services available to support students with disabilities that are specific to the state goals or programs.

How did this program benefit Mark? It helped him be comfortable with self-advocacy. This was really important for a variety of reasons. Should there have been an emergency at school, by the time we could have gotten there to help him, the crisis would have been over. That's not to say we wouldn't have been calling and texting, but it would be physically impossible to get to him right away. His Learning Specialist helped him navigate a particularly rough roommate situation where he had to find a new place to live right before Thanksgiving. Finding an open space on a college campus at that point in the semester can be difficult. To the credit of Texas Tech and their housing department along with his Learning Specialist, this situation was made much easier. Another time, Mark's professor in the computer science department told him there was an internship at NASA he felt Mark was qualified for and that he'd like to see him pursue it. Mark went to his Learning Specialist, and they devised a plan that involved coordinating with the career center on campus and extensive preparation or a series of interviews. The interviews were web-based, and because of the plan they developed and executed, Mark was able to handle them in a way that was well-prepared and allowed him to feel calm and less anxious. The team did such a good job preparing that he made it to the very last round of interviews—an accomplishment we are very proud of, as is he. Texas Tech requires that students to do a semester of study abroad. Mark worked with his Learning Specialist and the study abroad department to research what needed to be done in terms of applying for a passport, deadlines, scholarships, etc. He did a fabulous job of achieving this goal and spent most of the summer that year studying in Europe. If someone had said to my husband and I when he was a freshman that he would have a goal like this, we would have been skeptical. He carried this out flawlessly, made wonderful use of his time away, and had experiences he will treasure for the rest of his life. All of this because the program looked at him and said, "What does he need in order to achieve his goals?"

Mark's college experience reinforced for me that if a student is given the type of support they need, the chances of having a successful student complete and graduate with a degree are high.

Becoming a College Student! **by Mark**

I knew very early on that the life I wanted for myself wasn't a guarantee like it seemed for everyone else. Although I didn't have the words for it at first, I knew that the people around me lived at a level I didn't quite grasp. Things came naturally to them that I just couldn't match. When people asked what caused frustration in my life, I would tell them that it felt as if everyone else was in the professional leagues for a game I didn't know we had all decided to play.

It wasn't until I was a little older, around 12 or 13, that someone close to me learned about ASD, and I saw more and more similarities to myself with the more I learned. It wasn't long after that I was officially tested and diagnosed. I finally had a name and a reason for what made me feel different, and why what came so naturally to other people didn't for me. I knew clearly what I wanted out of life: to live the same life as other people and to form lasting connections and achieve what others knew they could. I wanted to live differently only in the ways that mattered to me as a person, not because it was already chosen for me. For a long time, I tried to achieve these goals with the tools I had, but without much luck. I knew that if this was the life that I wanted, something would have to change, and quickly. I was now in high school, and with college soon in my future, I decided I wanted to start the next phase of my life in as strong a place as I could.

I'll be always grateful that as all of this happened, I met the people whose impact would change my entire course. I found a mentor, and with his help I started to gain insights about myself and tools to make more genuine connections. Just as I was able to put this into practice, I met new people by chance who, although I didn't know it at the time, would become my deepest lifelong friends. As we grew to know each other, they came to know me, and for the first time I had people who accepted my differences and gave me guidance and a place to be vulnerable. I started to see a side of myself deep down that I didn't know I had: someone for whom all of the intangible things that had made me feel different came easily. As college came closer, I found a college with a program geared toward people on the spectrum like myself. Called CASE, it was a program at Texas Tech University that I was instantly drawn to for the way it would meet my needs individually, something that had been key to the momentum I was having. Knowing that I would have support as I started the next step gave me confidence that I could keep achieving my goals. Eventually it was time to move on to a new chapter, and the experiences I'd had showed me that growth I didn't know was possible could be in my future if I continued to work toward it.

At the start of my time in college, I had thought that this new chapter in my life would be one small step in a long journey. What I was met with was something unrecognizable. All at once I was a different person—something deep down I thought I'd never had came out. For the first time in my life, I forgot that I'd ever felt different from the people around me at all. Although only a short time ago I'd spend most of my time alone, with just a few close friends to break the solitude, suddenly I was surrounded by new friends and constantly having new experiences. I felt that I was doing all of the things that I was afraid that my differences would have made me miss out on. As all of this was happening, the CASE program at my college supported me in a better way than I could have imagined. I wanted to live a life to the same standards as the people around me, and my mentors in this program recognized this and gave me the tools to continue this. They saw me as a person at my own place in my journey, and not just someone who needed the exact same support as everyone who was a part of this program. Beyond the social side of college life, they also helped me navigate other issues such as roommate conflicts, talking to professors, and moving off campus; having support in planning helped to smooth a lot of the tougher moments of the college transition. With the support in college and back at home, I couldn't help but feel grateful for everything that had helped me make it this far.

As it goes, I did eventually have setbacks that challenged my goals. Relationships I had formed drifted apart, and were replaced by less healthy people. For the first time in a long time, I was doing things on my own while I regained my footing. During this time, the support of my mentors and my college program were invaluable; when I doubted if I had what it took to achieve the rest of my goals or to keep being the kind of person I had started to become, they gave me a space and tools to evaluate things and move forward. As I started to get my momentum back, I doubled my focus on achieving my goals and pushing myself as far as I could go with my support behind me. With the help and encouragement I had in planning, researching, and growing myself, I found myself more and more living the life I had always wanted to. In my time at college, I got the chance to travel internationally, interview with major science and tech companies, speak at disability conferences, and finish my degree while starting my dream career. All of these things I was only able to do because of both the validation I had from what I had already done, and the help that I received in making and executing the plans to make them all happen. I have my family, friends, mentors, and countless other supports through the years for making my younger self's dreams a reality that continues to grow.

I believe that we as neurodiverse people are not limited by what we think our capabilities are. The life I live now, and the person that I feel I am at my core, is something I spent much of my life believing was a future meant for different people than myself. The barriers that separated me from other people were real, but are now memories. I have a life that's every bit as rich and fulfilled as the people around me, something I thought for a long time would never be possible. I know that I'm fortunate in the place that I started from and the support I received in my journey, but I know as well that if I had resigned myself to be who I thought I was, I would never have learned that I am who I thought I could be.

Success

The parents and students we interviewed for this chapter seemed to have similar perspectives on what students would need to be successful in postsecondary education. They knew the importance of academics, but also the importance of having a social life and living independently on a college campus. Parents expressed comfort in knowing that these universities provided mentors, tutors, and advisors who could help their student achieve success. They chose universities that provided specific programs designed to address the needs of students with disabilities. In other words, the parents and students did their homework! Not all universities offer specific programs targeted for students with disabilities but do offer an array of services to help students become successful in their college journey.

Note that the students in this chapter had the support of their parents and were willing to consider their advice. This isn't always the case for many students. Not all support systems include families. Often students create support networks that include friends, case workers, classmates, professors, advisors, or other extended family members. A great deal of discussion ensued between these parents and their sons, and both sets of parents took the time to look for universities that had the level of services they felt their children required to achieve their goals. Although Ricky began at the community college level and Mark began at a 4-year university, they ended up in the same place—graduating with a college degree.

Final Thoughts

The information in this book is the result of progress that those in the field of education are slowly making in expanding the opportunities for students with LD and other disabilities to pursue a postsecondary education. College is a possibility! If you are a student with a disability, you can no longer assume that college is not an option.

Early planning and preparation is a key factor in a successful transition from high school to college. You can use this book as a guide to obtain the needed information and assist you in meeting the timelines along the way. If you need assistance with the process, talk with your parents, teachers, or a school counselor who can provide the additional support you may need to remain focused and on track.

As is evidenced throughout the book, it takes time and a commitment to fulfill all of the necessary requirements to get a letter of acceptance, but the work does not stop there. Granted, it is your decision whether or not you will disclose your disability to your college, but considering all of the changes that college brings, the continued support provided by the Student Disability Services Office can have a positive impact on your college experience. Just as your high school offered you support, colleges also are prepared to offer the necessary accommodations. Use them to your advantage. Those accommodations are only in place to level the playing field.

The following poem was written by Jacqueline Simpson, the president of the student chapter of Best Buddies at Oak Ridge High School in Conroe, TX. Students and faculty involved in organizations such as Best Buddies International can help facilitate friendships between students receiving special education services and peer buddies. As a peer buddy throughout high school, Jacqueline shared that she wanted her buddies to believe in themselves, whether it be in accomplishing a small goal or reaching a larger goal, and to know that going at your own pace will take you there. This was evidenced in many of the student responses from those interviewed throughout this book. It seems fitting to end our book with a reminder that the process to apply and then succeed in college is one that should be taken at your own pace and within your own comfort zone.

Progression
by Jacqueline Simpson

Life is neither a competition nor a race.
Your accomplishments need not surpass
those of others, nor must they be achieved
any quicker. For at first you cannot draw,
it is just as beautiful to merely color.

Remember, you are your own biggest advocate. Set goals and pursue them. Be prepared to change course. Ask questions. Seek answers. Follow through. Work hard and enjoy your life as a college student!

Glossary of Terms

Academic achievement: Refers to how a student is performing academically.

Academic advisor: A person on staff at the college or university who assists students in the development of their educational plan.

Accommodation: A modification to the delivery of instruction or method of student performance that does not significantly change the content or curriculum.

ACT: A college entrance exam that assesses high school students' general educational development and their ability to complete college-level work.

Advocacy: Speaking up for a cause, person, or idea.

Americans With Disabilities Act of 1990 (ADA): A civil rights law that provides equal access and opportunity and prevents discrimination for students with disabilities.

Assistive technology: Equipment, hardware, inventions, tools, or other assistance for people with disabilities; aids to help people do the tasks of daily life.

177

Attention Deficit/Hyperactivity Disorder (ADHD): A condition characterized by problems of inattention, hyperactivity, and/or impulsivity.

Autism spectrum disorders (ASD): A developmental disorder that affects a person's ability to socialize and communicate effectively with others.

Blackboard: An interactive online learning system designed to enhance teaching and learning through the use of software applications.

Career center: A resource area in a high school that will assist students in learning about careers and postsecondary institutions; many universities also have career centers for postcollege career advice and guidance.

College Board: A not-for-profit examination board that manages the administration of nationwide aptitude and achievement tests used by most U.S. colleges and universities as part of their admissions process.

Compensation strategies: Methods and techniques to provide students support in areas of deficits.

Course of study: An academic framework that includes the courses needed to complete a certification or degree program.

Daily living skills: The basic activities of daily living, such as self-care, work, homemaking, and leisure.

Disability Services Coordinator: A staff member on the college or university campus who assists the student in accessing the needed services for academic success.

Educational diagnosticians: Professionals who assess and diagnose the learning problems of students.

Equal Employment Opportunity Commission (EEOC): A federal agency in charge of administration and judicial enforcement of the federal civil rights laws.

Extracurricular activities: Student activities that are not part of the normal school curriculum; can include a range of clubs, organizations, and team sports.

Family Educational Rights and Privacy Act of 1974 (FERPA): A U.S. federal law that protects the confidentiality of student education records.

FO-LE

Four-year institution: A college, university, or postsecondary institution that provides students with a 4-year program of collegiate academic study.

Functional achievement: Refers to how a student is performing skills in daily living, personal and social interactions, and employability.

Functional vocational evaluation: An assessment process that is an organized approach to identifying the interests, needs, preferences, and abilities that an individual student has in the domain of occupational/ employability skills.

Grade Point Average (GPA): A student's cumulative grades.

Independent living: The ability to live on one's own.

Individualized Education Program (IEP): A written document that ensures that a child with a disability receives a free, appropriate education in the least restrictive environment; designed to meet the individual needs of a student with a disability.

Individuals With Disabilities Education Act (IDEA): A law ensuring services to children with disabilities throughout the nation; governs how states and public agencies provide early intervention, special education, and related services to more than 6.5 million eligible infants, toddlers, children, and youth with disabilities.

Instructional strategies: Methods, materials, and techniques that can be used to assist students in strengthening their areas of academic need, thereby enhancing the learning process.

Integrated employment: A job in which a person with disabilities has real work opportunities in a setting where most employees are nondisabled.

Learned helplessness: A person learns to act or behave helpless in a particular situation.

Learning disabilities (LD): A term that describes specific kinds of learning problems that affect a broad range of academic skills, including reading, writing, listening, speaking, mathematics, and reasoning abilities.

Learning styles: Conditions under which a student is most likely to learn; may be through a combination of any of the senses.

Letter of recommendation: A letter written by a teacher, counselor, or a well-respected community member who can talk about a student's personal qualities, accomplishments, and experiences that may have not been discussed in the student's college or job application.

Office for Civil Rights: A federal agency that prohibits discrimination in educational programs and activities receiving federal financial assistance.

Postsecondary education: Educational institutions beyond high school that have an academic, vocational, or professional focus.

Private college or university: A postsecondary school that is supported and run by a private agency; private schools typically charge higher tuition and have smaller enrollments than public schools.

Progress monitoring: Collecting and using data to frequently check students' progress toward success.

Public college or university: Postsecondary school that is supported by public funds; provides reduced tuition for students who are citizens of the state that supports it.

Related services: Services a student with disabilities needs in order to benefit from special education that may include, but are not limited to, speech therapy, physical therapy, and occupational therapy.

Research-based instructional strategies: Instructional strategies that have been proven through research to enhance student learning.

Resident assistant (RA): A trained leader within a college or university responsible for supervising students in a residence hall (dorm).

Response to intervention (RtI): An alternative method of identifying learning disabilities using early intervention, frequent progress monitoring, and intensive research-based instructional strategies.

SAT: A standardized test for admissions into U.S. colleges and universities; formerly known as the Scholastic Aptitude Test.

School psychologist: A psychologist who specializes in the assessment and problems of school-age children.

SE–VO

Section 504: A civil rights law that is part of the Rehabilitation Act of 1973; provides equal access and opportunity and prevents discrimination for persons with disabilities.

Self-advocacy: The ability to communicate one's talents, skills, and needed accommodations to others.

Self-determination: Enables individuals to take responsibilities for their lives at school and within the community.

Self-monitoring: Involves the student monitoring their own progress in the effort to develop a skill or complete a project.

Social skills: A set of social rules and regulations that people need to effectively communicate and interact with others.

Student Disability Services Office (SDSO): An office on the college or university campus that provides services and supports for students with disabilities; also referred to as Disability Services Office or Disability Support Services on some campuses.

Transition planning: The process of planning for a student's future as they move from high school into adult life.

Transition services: Services that include strategies and activities that will assist the student in preparing for postsecondary activities once they leave high school.

Two-year institution: Often referred to as a community college or junior college; provides students with a 2-year program of collegiate academic study.

U.S. Department of Justice: A department in the U.S. government designed to enforce the law, defend the interests of all Americans according to the law, and ensure fair and impartial administration of justice.

Vocational rehabilitation (VR) agency: Provides a variety of services that focus on career development, employment preparation, achieving independence, and integration in the workplace and community for people with disabilities.

Vocational training: Training at the high school or postsecondary level to provide students with work experience for future employment.

Resources

ACT.org

https://www.act.org

This site provides preparation and registration information regarding the ACT examination, including information for students with disabilities regarding accommodations to taking the test.

Association on Higher Education and Disability (AHEAD)

https://www.ahead.org

AHEAD is a professional membership organization for individuals involved in the development of policy and the provision of quality services to meet the needs of persons with disabilities involved in all areas of higher education. The website contains sections that focus on topics such as disability resources (best practices, civil rights laws, IDEA, universal design), students and parents, and special interest groups.

Career Key

https://www.careerkey.org

This site provides a career assessment that matches the student's personality with careers. It also includes information on how to judge career tests for credibility, career development, and educational options, and a career information blog.

College Board

https://www.collegeboard.org

Considered an inside source for college admission requirements, this site provides information for students and parents to assist in simplifying planning for college. Information on services for students with disabilities can be found at https://accommodations.collegeboard.org.

College Grazing

http://www.collegegrazing.com

This site is designed to assist students in finding a college that fits their needs and provides many interactive planning tools.

The Common Application

https://www.commonapp.org

The website is designed to make available services that support equity, access, and integrity in the college application process. It includes an online application used by many secondary schools to promote access by evaluating students using a holistic selection process.

Community Resources, Living Options & Residential Facilities, Transportation

https://www.heath.gwu.edu/community-resources-living-options-residential-facilities-transportation

Links with information in each of these areas can be found on this website. You may also submit a question to AskHEATH@gwu.edu.

Distance/Online Learning

https://www.heath.gwu.edu/distanceonline-learning

Resources with information pertaining to all aspects of distance/online learning are provided. The website also provides a guide to postsecondary online degree programs.

Division on Career Development and Transition (DCDT)

https://community.cec.sped.org/dcdt/home

A division of the Council for Exceptional Children, this organization promotes efforts to improve the quality of and access to career/vocational and transition services, as well as to increase the participation of education in career development and transition goals. The website contains several links to topics relevant to transition and planning. It also provides information regarding conferences and webinars.

DO-IT Disability, Opportunity, Internetworking, and Technology

https://www.washington.edu/doit/external-resource-topic/students-disabilities

The website serves to increase the successful participation of individuals with disabilities in challenging academic programs such as those in science, engineering, mathematics, and technology. Additionally, links to publications and information on children with disabilities, IDEA, and research-based instructional strategies are included.

Education Quest Foundation

https://www.educationquest.org

With a mission to improve access to higher education, the Education Quest Foundation provides a wealth of knowledge to be considered during the transition into college. The website offers free college planning and outreach services, as well as scholarship and grant information. The Students With Disabilities section (https://www.educationquest.org/11th-12th-grade-students/information-for-students-with-disabilities) addresses topics such as exploring career options, preparing for entrance exams, selecting a college, applying for admission and financial aid, self-advocacy, and your legal rights and responsibilities.

Educational Testing Service (ETS)

https://www.ets.org

Designed to advance the quality and equity in education, ETS provides assessments, research, and related services to students. This Disabilities and Health-related Needs page (https://www.ets.org/disabilities) presents information regarding testing accommodations for test takers with disabilities, including general information as well as accommodations for computer-based testing and paper-based testing. ETS also provides a wide range of information on various testing topics, including tips and resources for test takers.

Federal Student Aid

https://studentaid.ed.gov

This site provides information on financial aid services and is sponsored by the Federal Student Aid "Start Here Go Further" initiative.

Get Ready for College: A Resource for Teens With Disabilities

https://centerontransition.org/training/getready.cfm

This is an online course from the Center of Transition Innovations at Virginia Commonwealth University. This free, eight-session, self-paced course is designed to assist students in grades 9–12 in college readiness. In addition to the course, there is a wealth of additional information in the form of publications and resources.

HEATH Resource Center at the National Youth Transitions Center

https://www.heath.gwu.edu/repository

The HEATH Resource Center is a national clearinghouse that includes a repository containing updated information to help individuals with disabilities seek and obtain financial assistance for post-secondary education. The repository includes PDFs that describe federal financial aid programs, state vocational rehabilitation services, and regional and local sources.

How-To-Study.com

https://www.how-to-study.com

This site addresses the development of study skills, with information on SAT test-taking tips, essay tests, study groups, and study habits, among many other topics. There also are sections that address college planning and college success. The site offers study skills programs and guides in both English and Spanish.

LD OnLine: College and College Prep

http://www.ldonline.org/indepth/college

This site provides information on college preparation for students with learning disabilities.

National Center for Learning Disabilities (NCLD)

https://www.ncld.org/what-we-do/ya-initiatives

Working to ensure children, adolescents, and adults with learning disabilities have every opportunity to succeed in school, work, and life, NCLD provides information to parents and students regarding many aspects of learning disabilities. Young Adult Initiatives focuses on empowering young adults with learning and attention issues to build their leadership skills, protect their rights, and inspire others.

National Parent Center on Transition and Employment

https://www.pacer.org/transition/learning-center/postsecondary/preparing-for-postsecondary.asp

Resources are provided to assist parents in supporting the transition goals for students with disabilities, including career exploration, information on campus tours, and videos of students speaking about their transition experiences.

Online Colleges, Scholarships, and Degree Programs

https://www.college-scholarships.com

This site provides easy access to information about colleges and universities located across the U.S., free scholarship and financial aid searches, SAT and ACT test prep tips, and online degrees and distance learning. It contains a directory of pertinent college and university information, such as links to homepages, admission office email addresses and phone numbers, and links to online applications.

Smart About College

https://www.smartaboutcollege.org

Smart About College provides students and families with information necessary to prepare for postsecondary education. Topics covered include getting into and paying for college. Also included in this site are free ACT and SAT practice tests.

Think College

https://thinkcollege.net

Think College is a national organization dedicated to developing, expanding, and improving inclusive higher education options for people with intellectual disabilities. Think College supports evidence-based and student-centered research and practice by generating and sharing knowledge, guiding institutional change, informing public policy, and engaging with students, professionals and families.

U.S. Department of Education, Office for Civil Rights: Students With Disabilities Preparing for Postsecondary Education

https://www2.ed.gov/about/offices/list/ocr/transition.html

Information is provided to assist parents and students with disabilities regarding their rights and responsibilities during the transition process. In addition, a transition guide was developed to provide high school educators with answers to questions students with disabilities may have as they get ready to move to the postsecondary education environment (https://www.ed.gov/about/offices/list/ocr/transitionguide.html).

Wrightslaw

https://www.wrightslaw.com

Designed to provide up-to-date information about special education law and advocacy, this site contains articles, cases, newsletters, and resources on many topics of importance to parents. Sections found on this site include Training Programs, Publications, Advocacy Library, and Law Library. The site also contains information regarding transition services to education, work, or independent living.

References

American Psychiatric Association. (2013). *Diagnostic and statistical manual of mental disorders* (5th ed.). https://doi.org/10.1176/appi.books.9780890425596

Americans With Disabilities Act of 1990, 42 U.S.C. § 12102 *et seq.* (1990). https://www.ada.gov/pubs/adastatute08.htm

Bashir, A. S., Goldhammer, R. F., & Bigaj, S. J. (2000). Facilitating self-determination abilities in adults with LDD: Case study of a postsecondary student. *Topics in Language Disorders, 21*(1), 52–67.

Berger, S. L. (2014). *College planning for gifted students: Choosing and getting into the right college* (Updated ed.). Prufrock Press.

Brinckerhoff, L. C., Shaw, S. F., & McGuire, J. M. (2001). Promoting access, accommodations, and independence for college students with learning disabilities. *Journal of Learning Disabilities, 25*(7), 417–429. https://doi.org/10.1177/002221949202500702

Bruns, E. J., & Walker, J. S. (2010). The wraparound process: An overview of implementation essentials. In E. J. Bruns & J. S. Walker

(Eds.), *The resource guide to wraparound*. National Wraparound Initiative.

Chambers, C. R., Wehmeyer, M. L., Saito, Y., Lida, K. M., Lee, Y., & Singh, V. (2007). Self-determination: What do we know? Where do we go? *Exceptionality, 15*(1), 3–15.

Cimera, R. E., Burgess, S., & Bedesem, P. L. (2014). Does providing transition services by age 14 produce better vocational outcomes for students with intellectual disability? *Research and Practice for Persons with Severe Disabilities, 39*(1), 47–54. https://doi.org/10. 1177/1540796914534633

College Board. (n.d.). *Disability documentation guidelines*. https://acco mmodations.collegeboard.org/documentation-guidelines/disa bility-documentation

Covey, S. R. (1989). *The 7 habits of highly effective people*. Free Press.

Eckes, S. E., & Ochoa, T. A. (2005). Students with disabilities: Transitioning from high school to higher education. *American Secondary Education, 33*(3), 6–20.

EDsmart. (2016). *The future of distance learning*. https://www.edsm art.org/the-history-and-future-of-distance-learning

The Eleanor and Charles Garrett Center on Transition and Disability Studies at Sam Houston State University. (2020). *Postsecondary education: What students with disabilities and their families need to know* (3rd ed.).

Family Educational Rights and Privacy Act of 1974, 20 U.S.C. § 1232g (1974). https://www2.ed.gov/policy/gen/guid/fpco/ferpa/index. html

Field, S., Sarver, M. D., & Shaw, S. F. (2003). Self-determination: A key to success in postsecondary education for students with learning disabilities. *Remedial and Special Education, 24*(6), 339–349. https://doi.org/10.1177/07419325030240060501

Getzel, E. E., & Thoma, C. A. (2008). Experiences of college students with disabilities and the importance of self-determination in higher education settings. *Career Development for Exceptional Individuals, 31*(2), 77–84. https://doi.org/10.1177/0885728808317658

Getzel, E. E., & Wehman, P. (2005). *Going to college: Expanding opportunities for people with disabilities.* Brookes.

Gil, L. A. (2007). Bridging the transition gap from high school to college: Preparing students with disabilities for a successful postsecondary experience. *Teaching Exceptional Children, 40*(2), 12–15. https://doi.org/10.1177/004005990704000202

HEATH Resource Center at the National Youth Transitions Center. (2006). *Guidance and career counselors' toolkit: Advising high school students with disabilities on postsecondary options.* George Washington University. https://www.heath.gwu.edu/sites/g/files/zaxdzs2346/f/downloads/Toolkit%202014.pdf

HEATH Resource Center at the National Youth Transitions Center. (2015). *Planning ahead: Financial aid for students with disabilities.* The George Washington University. https://www.heath.gwu.edu/sites/g/files/zaxdzs2346/f/2015_FinAid-FINAL_508.pdf

Henrickson, J. M., Woods-Groves, S., Rodgers, D. B., & Datchuk, S. (2017). Perceptions of students with autism and their parents: The college experience. *Education and Treatment of Children, 40*(4), 571–596. https://doi.org/10.1353/etc.2017.0025

Horowitz, S. H., Rawe, J., & Whittaker, M. C. (2017). *The state of learning disabilities: Understanding the 1 in 5.* National Center for Learning Disabilities. https://www.ncld.org/research/state-of-learning-disabilities

Individuals With Disabilities Education Act, 20 U.S.C. §1401 *et seq.* (2004). https://sites.ed.gov/idea/statuteregulations

Joshi, G. S., & Bouck, E. C. (2017). Examining postsecondary education predictors and participation for students with learning disabilities. *Journal of Learning Disabilities, 50*(1), 3–13. https://doi.org/10.1177/0022219415572894

Kauffman, J., Hallahan, D. P., & Pullen, P. C. (Eds.). (2017). *Handbook of special education* (2nd ed.). Routledge.

Learning Disabilities Association of America. (2013). *Transition planning requirements of IDEA 2004.* https://ldaamerica.org/wp-content/uploads/2015/03/Transition-Planning.pdf

Lightfoot, A., Janemi, R., & Rudman, D. L. (2018). Perspectives of North American postsecondary students with learning disabilities: A scoping review. *Journal of Postsecondary Education and Disability, 31*(1), 57–74.

Madaus, J. W. (2005). Navigating the college transition maze: A guide for students with learning disabilities. *Teaching Exceptional Children, 37*(3), 32–37. https://doi.org/10.1177/00400599050370030

Marek, C. I., Wanzer, M. B., & Knapp, J. L. (2009). An exploratory investigation of the relationship between roommates' first impressions and subsequent communication patterns. *Communication Research Reports, 21*(2), 210–220. https://doi.org/10.1080/0882 4090409359982

Martin, J. E., Mithaug, D. E., Cox, P., Peterson, L. Y., Van Dycke, J. L., & Cash, M. E. (2003). Increasing self-determination: Teaching students to plan, work, evaluate, and adjust. *Exceptional Children, 69*(4), 431–447. https://doi.org/10.1177/001440290306900403

Martin, J. E., Van Dycke, J. L., Christensen, W. R., Greene, B. A., Gardner, J. E., & Lovett, D. L. (2006). Increasing student participation in IEP meetings: Establishing the self-directed IEP as an evidence-based practice. *Exceptional Children, 72*(3), 299–316. https://doi.org/10.1177/001440290607200303

Mason, C. Y., McGahee-Kovac, M., & Johnson, L. (2004). How to help students lead their IEP meetings. *TEACHING Exceptional Children, 36*(3), 18–24. https://doi.org/10.1177/004005990403600302

Massachusetts Department of Higher Education. (2019). *Undergraduate admissions standards for the Massachusetts State University system and the University of Massachusetts: Reference guide: 2019.* https:// www.mass.edu/foradmin/admissions/documents/DHEAdmissions StandardsReferenceGuide_2019.pdf

McCarthy, D. (2007). Teaching self-advocacy to students with disabilities. *About Campus, 12*(5), 10–16. https://doi.org/10.1002/ abc.225

McGuire, J. M., & Shaw, S. F. (1987). A decision-making process for the college-bound learning disabled student: Matching learner, institution, and support program. *Learning Disability Quarterly, 10*(2), 106–111. https://doi.org/10.2307/1510217

Nadeau, K. (2006). *Survival guide for college students with ADHD or LD* (2nd ed.). Magination Press.

National Center for Education Statistics (2019). *Fast facts: Distance learning.* https://nces.ed.gov/fastfacts/display.asp?id=80

National Collegiate Athletic Association. (n.d.). *Student-athletes with disabilities.* https://www.ncaa.org/about/resources/inclusion/student-athletes-disabilities

National Joint Committee on Learning Disabilities. (2007). The documentation disconnect for students with learning disabilities: Improving access to postsecondary disability services. *Learning Disability Quarterly, 30*(4), 265–274. https://doi.org/10.2307/25474638

Newman, L. (2005). Postsecondary education participation of youth with disabilities. In M. Wagner, L. Newman, R. Cameto, N. Garza, & P. Levine (Eds.), *After high school: A first look at the postschool experiences of youth with disabilities. A report from the National Longitudinal Transition Study-2* (NLTS2, pp. 4-1–4-16). SRI International.

PACER's National Parent Center on Transition and Employment. (n.d.). *Self-determination.* https://www.pacer.org/transition/learning-center/independent-community-living/self-determination.asp

PACER's National Parent Center on Transition and Employment. (2016). *Online college programs: Questions to consider for students with disabilities.* https://www.pacer.org/transition/resource-library/publications/NPC-51.pdf

Palmer, A. (2006). *Realizing the college dream with Autism or Asperger syndrome: A parent's guide to student success.* Kingsley.

Quinn, P. O., Ratey, N. A., & Maitland, T. L. (2000). *Coaching college students with AD/HD: Issues and answers.* Advantage Books.

Sandler, M. (2008). *College confidence with ADD: The ultimate success manual for ADD students, from applying to academics, preparation to social success and everything else you need to know.* Sourcebooks.

Scott, S. S. (1991). A change in legal status: An overlooked dimension in the transition to higher education. *Journal of Learning*

Disabilities, 24(8), 459–466. https://doi.org/10.1177/00222194
9102400803

Section 504 of the Rehabilitation Act, 29 U.S.C. § 706 *et seq.* (1973).

Sitlington, P. L., Neubert, D. A., & Clark, G. M. (2009). *Transition education and services for students with disabilities* (5th ed). Pearson.

Snyder, T. D., de Brey, C., & Dillow, S. A. (2016). *Digest of education statistics 2015* (NCES 2016-014). National Center for Education Statistics. https://nces.ed.gov/pubs2016/2016014.pdf

Taymans, J. M. (n.d.). *Selecting a college for students with learning disabilities or Attention Deficit Hyperactivity Disorder.* LD Online. http://www.ldonline.org/article/Selecting_A_College_for_Students_with_Learning_Disabilities_or_Attention_Deficit_Hyperactivity_Disorder

Thompson, S. J., Morse, A. B., Sharpe, M., & Hall, S. (2005). *Accommodations manual: How to select, administer, and evaluate use of accommodations for instruction and assessment of students with disabilities* (2nd ed.). Council of Chief State School Officers. https://osepideasthatwork.org/node/109

U.S. Department of Education. (n.d.-a). *College- and career-ready standards.* https://www.ed.gov/k-12reforms/standards

U.S. Department of Education. (n.d.-b). *Transitioning students with disabilities to higher education: attitude and self-advocacy.* LD Online. http://www.ldonline.org/article/Transitioning_Students_with_Disabilities_to_Higher_Education%3A_Attitude_and_Self-Advocacy

U.S. Department of Education, Office for Civil Rights. (2011a). *Students with disabilities preparing for postsecondary education: Know your rights and responsibilities.* https://www2.ed.gov/about/offices/list/ocr/transition.html

U.S. Department of Education, Office for Civil Rights. (2011b). *Transition of students with disabilities to postsecondary education: A guide for high school educators.* https://www2.ed.gov/about/offices/list/ocr/transitionguide.html

Van-Belle, J., Marks, S., Martin, R., & Chun, M. (2006). Voicing one's dreams: High school students with developmental disabilities learn about self-advocacy. *TEACHING Exceptional Children, 38*(4), 40–46. https://doi.org/10.1177/004005990603800406

Virginia Department of Education. (2003). *Virginia's college guide for students with disabilities.* http://www.doe.virginia.gov/special_ed/transition_svcs/college_planning/college_guide.pdf

Wehmeyer, M. L. (2002). *Self-determination and the education of students with disabilities.* Council for Exceptional Children.

Wehmeyer, M. L., & Palmer, S. B. (2003). Adult outcomes for students with cognitive disabilities three years after high school: The impact of self-determination. *Education and Training in Developmental Disabilities, 38*(2), 131–144.

Williams, J., & Bloom, B. (n.d.). *Top ten mistakes to avoid during post secondary transition planning/evaluation* [Unpublished whitepaper]. Council of Parent Advocates and Attorneys.

Wolanin, T. R., & Steele, P. E. (2004). *Higher education opportunities for students with disabilities: A primer for policymakers.* The Institute for Higher Education Policy.

Workforce Innovation and Opportunity Act, Pub. L. No. 113–128 (2014). https://www.congress.gov/bill/113th-congress/house-bill/803

Appendix

What Students With Disabilities and Their Families Need to Know

The following frequently asked questions and tips are adapted from the Eleanor and Charles Garrett Center on Transition and Disability Studies at Sam Houston State University. These questions address what students with disabilities and their families need to know about postsecondary education.

Postsecondary Education

Note. When we say the word *college*, it is all-inclusive. We mean all postsecondary education, including college, university, trade school, technical school, community college, and junior college!

Q: I won't get help in college, trade school, technical school, or universities. Should I go to college?

1. That statement is incorrect. Learn about disability services in higher education. All federally funded institutions of higher education are required to provide supports for students with disabilities.

2. Colleges are graded by their state; this is referred to as accountability ratings. Students who fail and drop out count against the university. That means there are more supports than disability services. Most colleges have academic, social, medical health, and mental health supports for all students, including students with disabilities.

3. Don't set limits for yourself. Many students with your disability have attended college, including students with intellectual disabilities (https://thinkcollege.net).

4. Try it; you just might like it.

5. Should you go to a technical college, community college, or university? That depends upon your final goal for employment. If the goal is a job that requires a certificate, like welding or being a medical technician, investigate the local community college or trade school. If you want to be a teacher or law enforcement officer, investigate both the community college and university. You can start at the university or begin at the community college and transfer to the university.

6. Should you go away to school or stay at home and attend a local college? That often depends on finances and personal responsibility of the students. Parents, most 18-year-old students are not prepared to leave home. Think hard about this one.

Q: Where do I go to find the help?

1. Colleges, universities, and technical schools have offices for students with disabilities.

200

2. Make an appointment and visit the colleges or universities you are interested in attending.
3. Visit the admissions office and the office for students with disabilities. Tour the campus.
4. Many postsecondary institutions have a welcome center and provide tours of the campus. You do not need to wait for the high school to plan college day visits.
5. Documentation of disability is required. Each institution is different. Call the office of disability services.
6. Shop around! Every postsecondary institution is different. You may like a college but find that the staff of the office of disability services are rigid or not person-centered with students with disabilities. On the other hand, you may find that when visiting disability services at your second or third choice of colleges, you walk out feeling like the staff believe in you and the supports they have will help you; that college may be the better choice. Remember, the goal is to complete the program, certificate, or degree. Attend the college that is a good match for you, your career goals, and the supports you need in order to be successful.

Q: What about admissions requirements?

1. In many states, students must graduate with endorsements and meet College- and Career-Ready Standards to attend public colleges as an incoming freshman. Contact the admissions office of the colleges you are interested in and ask about these requirements. Also ask if there are exceptions or exemptions. Call more than once. Some employees are more knowledgeable than others.
2. Students graduating on the state minimum plan may enter as a freshman at a community college or trade/technical school and later transfer to a university if that is the goal.
3. Some colleges have more admission requirements than others. Do your homework.

4. Some colleges look at the state assessment scores, SAT, and ACT scores. Some colleges look for more than scores. They want to know grade point averages. Did the student participate in high school clubs? Was the student an officer in the club, even if it was Scrapbook Chair? Did the student have a job while in high school? Was the job related to the career goal? Most colleges now understand that the well-rounded student is most likely to be successful, not the one with only high test scores on the SAT and ACT. In fact, some colleges are eliminating those scores from the application requirements.

5. Students who do not score at the required level of the state assessments (above the minimum pass rate), the ACT, or the SAT may be required to take a college placement test. This varies at each community college. For college-bound students, the college test or pretest can be used as a transition assessment, such as ACCUPLACER.

6. Some schools have a formula for admission, and testing is only part of the requirement.

7. Your resume of work experience, extracurricular activities, and references is important.

Q: What if I can't pass the entry tests?

1. Most colleges and universities require a type of placement tests if the state assessment score, ACT, or SAT are below certain numbers.

2. If you are participating in a certification program, many do not require the college entry exams, so whatever your score was is a moot point. Again, check with disability services and the college admissions office.

3. The most common placement tests are ACCUPLACER or Compass. Some states have their own predictive assessments. For example, in Texas many postsecondary institu-

tions administer the Texas Success Initiative Assessment (TSIA).

4. Some assessments are paper/pencil and some are computer versions.

5. What if I don't pass these tests? Most colleges have a pathway for students who do not pass the assessment(s). It may include participation in developmental, remedial courses. If that is the case, do not let it discourage you. Keep your goal in sight. This is simply one hurdle. Remember, there is more than one way to get to your high school. You can drive, ride the school bus, ride your bicycle, walk, or ride in a carpool. That is a life lesson. There are many ways to navigate the requirements to enter college and obtain certificates and degrees. Do your homework if you really want to do this. It is more about doing your homework then it is about the disability!

Q: Are there exemptions if you don't pass the tests?

1. Not really, but there are some exceptions that vary from college to college. Check with the disability services at each of the colleges you are interested in attending.

2. What are developmental classes? These are remedial classes, and the subjects are typically math, reading, and writing. You only take the class you need. If you did well on the math test but not on the reading and writing tests, you only take the reading and writing developmental classes.

3. What if I don't pass the developmental classes? Again, talk with the disability services and talk to more than one college. They all vary.

Q: Okay, so I make it to college. Then what?

1. Self-identify at the college's disability services office. (The name of the office that serves students with disabilities is

not the same at each college. It could be Office of Disability Services, Student Accessibility Services, etc.)

2. Parents can't help you on this one. Your parent can go with you, but college personnel will talk to you and will only talk with your parent if you give permission.

3. Yes, parents, we know you may be paying the college bills. It does not matter. If your future student is 18 years old or older, your child is a legal adult, and the law will only allow the college to communicate with you if your child grants permission. It's the law.

4. Students, this is your life—take charge!

5. Enroll and apply at the disability services office.

6. Ask your special education teacher or transition specialist at your high school to help you apply for disability services.

7. Once you are accepted as a client of the college office of disability services, ask the mentor assigned to you to help you find a good academic advisor for your certificate or degree program. You are trying to "stack the deck" in your favor to be successful. You try to find a good doctor, right? You seek out a good technology specialist when you have computer problems, right? Just anyone won't do! So, why not seek out a good academic advisor at your college? Then you will have great advice and mentoring from both the college disability services and your academic advisor.

Q: Can I afford to go?

1. Students and parents, you need to talk about how college will be funded.

2. If students and parents do not have money for college, this does not mean a student cannot attend college. There are many ways to fund postsecondary education.

3. If you are a junior, talk with the Vocational Rehabilitative (VR) representative on your high school campus to obtain

information about supports available to go to college. Be ready to apply at the beginning of your senior year.

4. If you are a senior, apply *now* with VR Services at the Workforce Commission in your state. The transition specialist at your high school or district can help you apply for VR eligibility. Why do you want to apply for VR Services? Because if you qualify, VR Services may provide financial assistance for books, tuition, and possibly more.

5. *Do not* get so busy during your senior year that you do not have everything decided and in place prior to graduation. Try to have everything completed by December.

6. If you do not have the VR application and acceptance completed before graduation, chances are really good that *you will not have the books and tuition from VR for the fall semester!* You will have to pay for college yourself and try again in the fall to apply for VR funds for the next semester in the spring. Agencies take a long time to process application paperwork, and most slow down and take vacation, too.

7. Parents, almost all colleges require student to first apply for federal financial aid in order to qualify for financial assistance from other sources. Yes, you will be required to put your income from your last tax statement in the application. Many students who could have had financial assistance were not able to attend college because their parents refused to fill in the parent income box. Don't be that parent. Help your child obtain eligibility.

8. Check with the financial aid office at the college or university. They will also have information.

9. Apply for scholarships. You would be surprised at how much money is never given out because no one applied. Check with the program you want to attend. Sometimes each program has additional scholarships that are not listed with your high school and not even listed in the scholarship office at the college you want to attend. Check with the local chamber. Check with the Lions Club International. Money is out there!

Q: What if college is too hard?

1. You are not your disability.
2. You will not be the only person who may struggle academically, so don't blame the disability.
3. Organize your resources. Visit the college academic support center for all students and the office for students with disabilities. Many programs offer tutorials, and you can also join clubs and organizations. Most programs have academic supports for students, such as tutorials, study buddies, etc.
4. Use your resources. If you have support resources and don't use them, then failure is not related to your disability, but to a lack of self-discipline and self-determination.
5. Don't quit when the going gets tough. Anyone who went to college will tell you they struggled, some more than others. They will also tell you that the difference between them and the ones who did not make it is that they didn't quit!
6. Recognize problems before it is too late and use your resources to solve the problem.

Q: College education is more than books?

1. Attend the new student orientation.
2. Become part of the college.
3. Join organizations that interest you. There are many, such as the Agriculture Club; the African Student Association; the Theater Troupe; the Student Advisory Board for Diversity, Equity, and Inclusion; the National Organization of Hispanics in Criminal Justice; the Student Council for Exceptional Children (future teachers); Collegiate FFA; Baptist Student Union; Episcopal Student Center; Catholic Student Center; and many more.
4. Organizations support their members because they care about them and do not want to lose them if they flunk out of college. Many organizations support their members through

study groups, in addition to social events and activities to build leadership skills.

5. Get involved with student government. Just because you were not involved in high school does not mean you can't be involved in college. Start as a student government volunteer and learn how to join the leadership ranks.

6. Join a sorority or fraternity. They also have academic support activities because the Panhellenic Council ranks the organization according to academic success as well as the traditional Greek attributes. They actually do a great job with supporting freshmen with required study hours, tutorials, etc.

7. Balance the classes with getting involved in the college life. Don't take overload yourself with classes. Don't take multiple hard classes in one semester. Have your mentor in disability services and your academic advisory guide you. If it takes you an extra semester, that is okay. The goal is to learn to be a successful adult and graduate.

Q: What type of help can I expect from disability services?

1. It depends on the college or university. Again, visit more than one college.

2. First visit the college you do *not* want to attend. What? That's right. College is new for you and has changed since the adults in your life attended. You may not know what to expect, what you will learn, or the questions to ask. That is why you visit the college(s) you are least interested in attending first. You will be able to listen. You will learn the questions you need to ask. You will be better prepared to investigate the colleges you do want to attend by using the "doing your homework" method.

3. Some of the more common supports are:
    a. A quiet place to take tests.

b. Having tests read to you or technology with text-to-speech features.

c. Note-taking assistance or an electronic pen or device that enables you to record and transfer the recording to your computer, which will change the voice to text.

d. Tutoring and study groups.

e. Other supports, including priority registration, extended time for assignments, extended time for taking tests, audiobooks, peer support groups, and more.

Entitlement Versus Non-Entitlement

1. Students, college is *not* public school. Your success is up to you and your ability to create a support system for yourself and use it!

2. No one will come to see if you need help. No one will change the outcome if you "did not think you would need help," "did not want to tell them you had a disability," "did not want your parent to be mad," or "did not know the disability services existed." *It is all up to you!*

3. Don't wait until the last minute to do your homework on supports available at the college you want to attend. Begin in your junior year of high school. Finish in your senior year.

4. The college experience won't find you. You must find it and grab on! It is easier to stay in college and not quit if you are enjoying the experience, have a support system, and making progress toward your goals.

Attitude Goes a Long Way

1. Everyone in college experiences some problems.
2. Don't look at the challenges through disability eyes.
3. You are you! You are not your disability!
4. Know the difference between a feeling and a fact.

5. Use positive self-talk.
6. Use the resource network you put together. Add more resources if needed.

The Role of the Parent at the College of a Student With a Disability

1. There isn't one!
2. Parents, again, your child is considered a legal adult, and therefore the college will not talk to you without your child's permission. Even then, the college will respond to the answers your child gives and not yours.
3. Parents who pay for their child's education are no more entitled to information and participation than parents who do not pay.
4. Parents whose child has a disability are no more entitled to information and participation than parents whose child does not have a disability.
5. Parents, your role is encourager, mentor, and emotional supporter for your child. If you are also able to financially support them, great, but the first role is more important.
6. Parents, students do not have to have a disability to fail a college class or flunk out of college. Don't panic if your child is barely getting by—they are trying! Encourage them. With each day, they will become older, wiser, and more mature, and will have a better chance of passing in the future.
7. *One thing parents can do:* As mentioned earlier, students with disabilities may apply for funding for books and tuition to attend college. If the student attends a trade/technical school, VR Services may also assist with tools, etc. Eligibility is not a guarantee!
   a. The student must meet with VR and complete the application in the senior year prior to graduation. You can still apply as a college student. The office for disability ser-

vices will provide you with the contact information. But remember, you have to pay the bill during the semester while you wait for the application to process, so apply in high school if you can.

b. The application is not complete until the parent component is completed and signed, and the application is submitted. That includes parent income information unless the child is an emancipated adult. In that case, they are not a dependent on the parent's income taxes.

c. The eligibility is not determined until both the student and parent have completed their responsibilities in the application process.

d. *Many* students with disabilities do not receive money from VR for books and tuition because the parent did not complete their part of the requirements. Parents and students thought just meeting with VR and filling out the paperwork was "all there was." *Finish the process!*

College and Family Medical Insurance

1. Parents, check with your family medical insurance before your child goes off to college to find out the requirements for your child to remain on the family medical insurance policy.
2. Most family medical policies will remain in effect for the child who graduates from high school and goes to college. If the child must be a full-time student, for most colleges that is 12 credit hours per semester, depending on the institution. However, there is an exception if the child needs to take fewer hours due to the disability.
3. Many family medical policies will remain in effect if the student submits a letter to the insurance from a doctor or the college office of disability services that states the student is unable to take the full load due to the disability. It is not a

sure thing, but most of the time this is accepted to validate a reduced course load.

4. Parents, while your child is in high school, began to teach them to be responsible for medications, calling the doctor's office to schedule an appointment, and picking up prescriptions. Their first time at college is not the time to learn these adult activities.

Next Steps

1. The importance of IEP meetings to plan transition services:
   a. Check with the high school counselor, special education diagnostician, and special education case manager to be sure you are on track for graduation.
   b. Discuss your plans for postsecondary education in your IEP meeting.
   c. Discuss ways to ensure your IEP will put you on track to graduate from college and be prepared for postsecondary education.

2. Transition assessments to develop the IEP should include assessments for students with postsecondary education goals. Transition assessments related to postsecondary education may include, but are not limited to: time management, learning styles, community access, self-determination skills, pretest for the ACCUPLACER or another college readiness assessment required in your state, and medical/health awareness.

3. Check out the college, university, or technical schools you are interested in attending.

4. Shop around, do your homework, and visit more than one college!

5. Don't just investigate the college and talk to admissions. Visit the office of disability services to find out who works

there and if you get the impression they will want to help you.

Resources

- ACCUPLACER: https://www.accuplacerpracticetest.com
- "Education's Most Damaging 'Urban Legend'" by Rick Lavoie: http://www.ldonline.org/lavoie/7277
- Association of Higher Educations and Disability: https://www.ahead.org/home
- "The Top 5 U.S. and International Colleges for the Deaf" by Jamie Berke: https://www.verywellhealth.com/deaf-education -colleges-for-the-deaf-1048366
- National Federation of the Blind: https://www.nfb.org
- National Alliance on Mental Illness (NAMI), Teens and Young Adults: https://www.nami.org/Your-Journey/Teens-Young-Adults
- Think College: https://thinkcollege.net
- "Higher Education Resource Guide for Students With Disabilities" (English and Spanish) by the Texas Council for Developmental Disabilities: https://tcdd.texas.gov/resources/publications

Note. Adapted from "Postsecondary Education: What Students With Disabilities and Their Families Need to Know (3rd ed.)," by the Eleanor and Charles Garrett Center on Transition and Disability Studies at Sam Houston State University, 2020. Copyright 2020 by the Eleanor and Charles Garrett Center on Transition and Disability Studies. Adapted with permission.

About the Authors

Cynthia G. Simpson, Ph.D., has more than 25 years of experience in the public and private sector as a preschool teacher, special education teacher, elementary teacher, educational diagnostician, professor of education, and university administrator (Vice President of Academic Affairs/Provost). She maintains an active role in the lives of children and young adults with exceptionalities as an educational consultant in the areas of assessment, inclusive practices, and transition planning. Her professional responsibilities include serving on the Board of Directors for National Certification for Educational Diagnosticians and National Council for Accreditation of Teacher Education as well as serving as a state advisor to the Texas Educational Diagnostician Association. Cynthia has many publications to her credit (books and articles) and is a featured speaker at the international, national, and state level. Cynthia has won several awards and received numerous recognitions for her work with individuals with disabilities, as well as her contributions to the field of special education.

Vicky G. Spencer, Ph.D., has served in the field of special education for more than 20 years as a special education teacher, educational consultant, and assistant professor. She also has worked for the Virginia Department of Education, providing teacher training throughout the state focusing on a variety of academic areas dealing with students with special needs. Vicky continues to remain actively involved in the field as she collaborates with special education teachers to implement cognitive strategies within the inclusive classroom setting. Her current research interests include cognitive strategy instruction for students with mild to moderate disabilities, autism, and transition planning. Vicky has presented findings from her research at state, national, and international conferences and published numerous articles that disseminate those findings. Vicky currently is an associate professor and the Director for the Applied Behavior Analysis Program at Shenandoah University, Winchester, VA.

Printed in the United States
by Baker & Taylor Publisher Services